Dangerous, Black, and Notorious

America's First Self Made Female Millionaire

Woody R. Clermont

**Dangerous, Black, and Notorious: America's
First Self Made Female Millionaire**

© 2025 Woody R. Clermont

Acknowledgments: The editor gratefully acknowledges the enduring legacy of Mary Ellen Pleasant, the Mother of Civil Rights in California. Thanks are due to family, friends, and colleagues whose encouragement made this story telling possible.

Contents

Contents

Part I

Prologue

MARY ELLEN PLEASANT, SAN FRANCISCO
(MODERN RESTORATION)

Chapter 1

A Billion in Shadows

Act I

The fog came first. It always did in San Francisco, pouring in from the Pacific like some ancient spirit, muffling the lamps, softening the brick of Nob Hill's rising mansions. By the time the mist reached the steep streets, it carried whispers with it: fragments of stories told in boardinghouses and barrooms, on the front steps of gilded hotels, even in the polished drawing rooms of bankers who believed they alone knew the pulse of money.

"Thirty million," someone would murmur, as if speaking the number too loud might conjure her. "Thirty million dollars in her grasp."

No name was needed. Everyone knew who *she* was. Mary Ellen Pleasant: the woman who had risen from nowhere, who had walked into the heart of a city still wild from gold and built an empire from things as ordinary as soap, meals, and lodging. She was called many things, businesswoman, abolitionist, madam, witch, but all the names circled the same burning core: power.

The papers printed her face in crude etchings, shading her cheekbones too dark, her eyes too sharp, her jaw too firm. They called her "Mammy Pleasant" with a cruel grin, as if shrinking her down with that word could make her less formidable. But those who saw her in person, striding the streets of San Francisco in silks, her hat tilted like a crown, felt something different. They said she carried herself as though she owned the sidewalks, as though the cobblestones themselves bent to her pace.

In parlors lit by gaslamps, gossip swirled thicker than smoke. The fortune was real, some insisted. Hadn't she financed railways? Didn't she hold half the city's deeds in her name? They claimed her coin had once rattled in John Brown's pocket, sent east to stoke the fire of revolt. Yet others swore it was myth: an exaggeration born of fear. "No colored woman can hold thirty million dollars," a banker barked once, before sipping his brandy. But even as he said it, his eyes flicked to the shadows in the room, as if he feared her hand might already be on his accounts.

The legend traveled faster than any streetcar she fought to desegregate. Thirty million. Enough to crush a railroad baron. Enough to raise armies. Enough to place her among the wealthiest souls in the nation, if not the wealthiest woman in America, and certainly the only Black woman whispered of in such terms. The number itself became a talisman, carved into memory, repeated like a prayer or a curse. Thirty million. Thirty million. Thirty million.

And in that city of earthquakes and fortunes made overnight, the rumor was more than arithmetic. It was a story people needed to tell themselves about what was possible, and what was dangerous. A Black woman holding power on the scale of Vanderbilts and Astors? To some, it was a miracle. To others, an abomination.

So they gave her another name: "Voodoo Queen." When business rivals failed to topple her in court, when rumors of lawsuits and betrayals proved too ordinary to explain her endurance, they turned to darker explanations. She must command spirits. She must keep candles burning through the night, call on forces unseen. It was easier, perhaps, to imagine sorcery than to face the truth - that she was simply more cunning, more disciplined, more fearless than the men who despised her.

On Nob Hill, where the mansions of railroad kings gleamed like fortresses, they said she haunted the edges of their empire. They pictured her walking at dusk, her shadow falling across the gates, her wealth and her will pressing against their privilege. A woman who had been denied everything by the world, now rumored to possess more than all of them.

And through it all, Mary Ellen Pleasant said little. She let the rumors run like wildfire, let her enemies choke on their own inventions. When she spoke, it was with the precision of a blade - court testimony, contracts, instructions to her lawyers. The rest, she left to imagination. She knew what power was: not merely what you hold in your hand, but what others *believe* you hold.

So the fog rolled in, and the number gleamed like a lantern inside it: **$30,000,000.** Fact or phantom, it was enough. Enough to crown her in myth before the story even began.

Act II

The name came from the papers, ink dripping with malice: **"Mammy Pleasant."** They thought they had found the perfect word to contain her. A word that shrank her into a caricature, pressed her into the mold of the loyal servant, the harmless housekeeper. It was supposed to reduce her to a figure at the margins of power, apron tied, smile fixed, voice hushed.

But the nickname never fit. It clung awkwardly,

like a borrowed coat too small for her shoulders. In the drawings published in the *San Francisco Call*, her lips were drawn wide, her eyes exaggerated, the features sharpened into mockery. Readers chuckled, congratulating themselves that they had her measured. Yet when she walked through the actual streets, her silks rustling, her chin lifted, the laughter died on people's lips.

She rarely challenged the name in public. She wore it like a mask, knowing masks have uses. If the world insisted on calling her "Mammy," she could step into that role when it suited her, only to peel it away when the time came to reveal the sharper edge beneath.

And that mask served her well. Behind it, she managed her enterprises, shifted her holdings, whispered into the ears of politicians. The irony was sharp: in attempting to make her small, her enemies had only given her another layer of disguise.

In the grand parlors of Nob Hill, society women spoke her name with disdain, lowering their voices to a hiss. But the same women, behind closed doors, sought her aid, borrowed her money, asked her counsel. The mask made them think she was manageable. She knew otherwise.

The newspapers tried to strip her humanity with ink, but they could not erase the truth that she was a woman who had navigated slavery and freedom, secrecy and spectacle, business and betrayal. The name "Mammy Pleasant" became less an insult than a testament to the fact that she lived so far beyond the categories available to white San Francisco that they could only reach for the most tired, racist stereotype they had.

And still, the rumors of her wealth clung tighter than any nickname. Thirty million dollars. She could have bought and sold the very presses that printed their caricatures, the very mansions whose mistresses gossiped over tea. And perhaps that was what made the mask necessary for them. To admit her full self was too much. To imagine her fortune was too terrifying. So they gave her a costume, and in so doing, made her legend only grow.

Act III

The city was born in frenzy. San Francisco rose not like an oak but like a wildfire, sudden and voracious, devouring gold dust and spitting out mansions. In the 1840s, it was a huddle of tents and gambling halls; by the 1870s, it was Nob Hill, lined with palaces. Railroad kings carved their castles from quarried stone, chandeliers spilling light like rivers of flame. In drawing rooms, guests drank French champagne and traded tales of fortunes won and lost before the ink dried on the contracts.

But even in those halls, amid the marble staircases and gilded mirrors, her name was spoken.

Mary Ellen Pleasant. Not with respect, not with affection, always with a kind of wary fascination.

"She's clever," said one merchant, tugging at his waistcoat, "but she deals in shadows."

"She's dangerous," whispered a banker's wife, lowering her voice to a near hiss.

"She's worth thirty million," someone else muttered, and the room fell still.

The fortune clung to her reputation like perfume, sweet to some, noxious to others, always in the air. Thirty million dollars. In the city of instant riches, no figure loomed larger. The barons had their railroads, the silver kings their mines, but Pleasant's wealth was stranger, harder to trace. It came not from veins of ore or state-backed charters, but from a thousand smaller arteries, boardinghouses filled with miners, laundries that never ceased, kitchens that fed the hungry. She did not merely ride the wave of San Francisco's growth; she built the scaffolding on which it climbed.

And for that, she was both admired and feared.

The contrast was sharp. On Nob Hill, the Crockers, Huntingtons, and Stanfords entertained senators beneath gaslit ceilings twenty feet high.Pleasant, meanwhile, made her presence felt in subtler ways: a visit to a business office, a word with a lawyer, a hand in a contract. To some she seemed omnipresent, an invisible shareholder in ventures that shaped the city.

The great irony, whispered with relish in cigar smoke, was that she had begun in labor. Not as a baron, not as a prospector, but as a servant in her own establishments. She had scrubbed, cooked, and carried and from those modest beginnings built the empire that now frightened them. While men of standing stumbled under gambling debts, she quietly invested. While others squandered fortunes on whiskey and cards, she bought land.

It was almost worse, in their eyes, that she had not "earned" it in a manner they understood. Wealth, they believed, should be inherited, or at least forged from enterprises that required vast capital. But to rise from laundry tubs and kitchens, from the boardinghouses where miners coughed and cursed - that was indecent. It upset the order of things.

So they called her names. They drew her in grotesque lines. They muttered about voodoo. Anything to explain away the fact that a Black woman had carved a fortune in the very soil they thought belonged to them.

Still, some were shrewd enough to respect her, if only privately. There were whispers that certain barons consulted her quietly, borrowing coin, cutting deals through intermediaries. None of them would admit it in daylight, but more than one palace on Nob Hill stood partly on foundations her money had helped to pour.

The city itself seemed to reflect her contradictions. By day, San Francisco glimmered: white mansions against a blue sky, shop windows gleaming with imported goods. By night, the fog crept down like a cloak, and the gaslamps struggled against its weight. In that shifting world, half-bright, half-shadowed; Pleasant thrived. She knew how to vanish into a crowd, and she knew how to command a room. She walked between worlds: the drawing room and the kitchen, the courtroom and the alley.

Always, though, the number followed her. Thirty million. The gossip swelled with every telling, like a tide no one could hold back. It was repeated in the markets, in the churches, in the parlors, until it no longer mattered whether it was true. The city believed it, and that belief alone gave it teeth.

On Nob Hill, where marble and granite testified to the permanence of men who had only arrived two decades before, Pleasant's legend was the one thing they could not build away. They could sneer, they could sue, they could gossip. But they could not erase the idea that a woman they scorned walked beside them with a fortune that rivaled theirs.

And so the city itself became her stage. The rumble of streetcars, the chiming of church bells, the endless pounding of hammers building mansions: every sound carried the rumor forward. San Francisco was not merely a place she lived; it was the chorus that sang her name.

Act IV

They could not forgive her competence, so they named it sorcery.

In rooms lacquered with mahogany and self-importance, men took turns explaining Mary Ellen Pleasant to one another as if holding a séance. A decanter went around like a shared candle; stories were offered, warmed by breath, passed hand to hand until they caught. She had a room, they said, where no light dared settle. She kept bottles lined like soldiers, each labeled in a cramped, secret hand. She drew chalk symbols on the floor and stood inside them when she balanced accounts. She tied red thread around contracts before she signed.

Most of it was nonsense, of course: pretty lies lacquered over uglier truths, but rumor seldom asks permission of reality. If a servant glimpsed a candle burning late in a boardinghouse office, that became proof of ritual. If a ledger page showed neat columns that unnerved a man who had never kept his own books, that became "strange figures." If a note came folded from Pleasant to an attorney, sealed with a smear of dark wax, why, that was a charm, and the suit was already lost.

The city loved its ghost stories because they made the living easier to understand. A woman who moved money with quiet hands and unerring timing? A woman who had survived slavery and silence and the narrow corridors of respectability to reach the high balconies of wealth? That needed a supernatural footnote. Otherwise there would be nothing between the barons and the mirror.

And yet, admit this, Pleasant knew how to use a stage that others set for her. If a rumor said she lit candles at midnight, she did not rush to snuff the wick. If they said she whispered to spirits, she let the silence afterward deepen until men heard their own fear. If some claimed she could turn a judge's head with a look, she did not waste time arguing about optics; she prepared better paperwork.

That paperwork was its own ritual. Contracts in a clean, unsentimental hand. Deeds filed on time. Receipts kept like prayer beads. She believed in numbers because numbers could not be put out of a drawing room or refused at a train door. And while the city gorged itself on legends about jars of herbs and mumbled words, she learned the flavor of interest and the scent of a market about to turn.

Still, the Gothic novella wrote itself.

A reporter young, hungry, coat too thin for the fog, followed her once from a hearing. He kept to doorways, as if the stone could hide his intention. Pleasant did not look back; she didn't need to. She walked as the city's grade demanded, foot sure, hat as precise as punctuation. He told himself he was on the trail of the Voodoo Queen of San Francisco.

He would write about the wicked empire behind the silks, the candles guttering in a basement with no windows, the whispered bargains in the language of New Orleans nights.

Instead he watched her turn into a narrow office where lamps burned plainly and the only magic was ink. She read, conferred, signed. When she emerged, she nodded to the clerk who held the door - an old man whose fingers shook from the sea air and age, and asked after his rheumatism. The reporter forgot to lift his pencil. He had been promised thunderclouds and found barometer readings; he had expected a hex and stumbled on a schedule. The article he eventually wrote was inked with clichés anyway: witch, enchantress, shadows, but the crowd preferred his first draft in the bar where he boasted of what he almost saw. In the telling, the lamps dimmed, the clerk with rheumatism vanished, and a candle returned to her hand.

Another night the city claimed to see her on the steps of a mansion at the crown of Nob Hill. The tale said she stood there a long time, and the lord of that house drew the curtain back with two fingers, and their eyes met, his indignant, hers amused. The hill held its breath. Was it true? It doesn't matter. It was true that her name could cross a threshold that barred her body. It was true that the rumor of thirty million dollars moved through corridors uninvited. Wealth, whether counted or conjured by the mouth of others, is a key; the tumblers do not ask where the metal was mined.

Women told a different set of stories. A laundress swore that her cousin's cousin, taken ill, had received a parcel from Pleasant—a vial and a page of instructions—after which the fever receded like a tide. A seamstress said Pleasant touched the seam of her life with a quiet word and the landlord's cruelty loosened. A widow whispered that a small loan arrived, no interest required if she kept her house for three months and did not let despair sign her name. Did Pleasant send those parcels? Maybe. Perhaps the vial held vinegar and cloves and a reprimand to boil the water; perhaps the landlord was visited by an attorney who spoke in the cool language of contracts; perhaps the loan came from an account with no advertised name at all. But mercy is its own kind of spell, and no one should be surprised that the city called it magic when it arrived from hands they refused to see as equal.

The men preferred bloodier anecdotes. A partner betrayed her and found his horses refusing the bit. A rival laughed at her in court and tripped on the courthouse steps; his ankle swelled to the size of his pride. A judge wrote an opinion in impatient ink and discovered the words "reversed on appeal" stitched into the hem of his robe. The city embroidered the world to suit its taste. If Providence frowned at those who crossed her, well,

Providence was a stand-in for the mathematics of consequence, and mathematics kept wonderful ledgers.

Here is what can be proven and needs no candle: she kept a network. Information traveled to her from kitchens and carriages, from parlors and porters' lounges and the back pews of churches where gossip disguised itself as concern. She paid attention. She remembered who owed what, and who hurt whom, and which law could be bent like willow and which would break a man who leaned too hard. She time-stamped her compassion and her retaliation. She knew that a secret is a kind of currency, and that the city minted them hourly.

So when they accused her of calling spirits, perhaps they weren't wrong. She could summon, on a summer afternoon, the pale face of a banker who believed he had buried his mistake in winter. She could speak in quiet tones to a man's conscience until it looked like regret. She could appear where fear was already gathering like fog and give it shape. That is, after all, what a rumor does. And she was a mistress of rumor as other people are masters of mills.

Once, during a hearing where a carriage company pretended not to know the law, a lawyer joked too loud about her dark arts. Pleasant turned her head—only a fraction, the angle a queen gives a jester—and smiled without showing teeth. "You misunderstand me," she said later in the corridor, voice low enough that the plaster leaned in to hear. "I don't work in shadows. I work with clocks." The lawyer laughed as if he did not understand, which was wise. She had timed the filing, the witness, the appeal; midnight belonged to candles, but ten a.m. belonged to clerks, and they were the real spirits of the courthouse.

Witchcraft was a useful costume—like "Mammy," like "madam," like all the garments they tried to dress her in. She wore it when it kept hands off her. She dropped it in rooms where plain speech could earn interest. She understood that a city is a theater and that the door marked *Employees Only* is just another proscenium. The audience wants smoke; the stagehand wants a rope that does not fray.

And still, the $30,000,000 glowed behind every tale. The number lent weight to the fantastic. No one would bother inventing midnight rites for a woman with three dollars and a ledger. But for a fortune that could tilt a railroad? For a sum that could drag a company, heels digging, into the century where Black riders took any seat they paid for? Of course the city dressed its fear in nightclothes. Of course it heard drums where there were only boots and the press of a crowd and the heartbeat of a case.

What the stories never say is how tired one must

be to carry a legend like armor. How heavy the candle feels when the room expects lightning. How often the lamp of a clerk's desk is sorcery enough, and the ink dries on a judgment that makes the miraculous ordinary. The world prefers a hex to a habit. But habit breaks chains just the same.

So let them talk of bottles and chalk and thread. Let them set the scene: a woman in a room with late-burning light, the fog pressed to the window like a listening ear. Let them imagine she speaks to shadows. She does. The shadows have names: Precedent, Contract, Debt, Appeal, and when she calls, they come.

And when they come, they move the city.

The barons, who built their palaces on steam and steel, knew that movement is the only magic that counts. Rails across mountains; money across tables; signatures across lines. They sensed in her the same grammar, learned in different schools. That is why they feared and envied her. Not because she conjured phantoms, but because she learned their language and answered without apology.

Soon enough, the city would watch that language carved into decisions. Soon enough, a streetcar bell would ring like a small coin of freedom, and the rumor of sorcery would find itself face to face with the harder miracle of law obeyed. But here, in the last hush before the gavel, the tales still flicker and weave. Thirty million gleams like a charm in the pocket of the night. A woman moves through fog that parts for no one else. Candles burn. Ledgers breathe. The stage is set.

The next act begins in a courtroom.

Act V

The fog was thickest outside the courthouses. Maybe it only seemed that way because gossip clung to stone steps better than it did to the plank sidewalks of Market Street. Men in frock coats gathered in clusters, smoke curling from their cigars, watching as Mary Ellen Pleasant mounted those stairs. She did not hurry. She moved with a rhythm that made the crowd part even when they swore they would not yield an inch.

Inside, the air was always taut. Courtrooms in San Francisco were theater and battlefield both. Oak benches creaked under the weight of witnesses, clerks shuffled papers like card dealers, and lawyers rehearsed their indignation as though the jury box were an opera balcony. Judges puffed themselves up, believing their words fell like thunder. And then Pleasant would enter, her presence folding the noise down to a hush.

She was not there to beg. She was there to fight— sometimes with her money, sometimes with her words, always with the law.

One case cut through the years like a bright blade: **the streetcar suits.** Pleasant, along with other plaintiffs, pressed against the city's segregated lines. White San Franciscans wanted Black riders off their precious cars; conductors were instructed to toss them like baggage. Pleasant did not bow. She sued. Again and again, until the companies had to defend their prejudice in black ink and testimony.

Witnesses told the court she boarded cars with dignity, was ordered off, and still returned. Some described her standing firm, her eyes never lowering, her voice precise. If they called her "Mammy" on the platform, she let the insult fall and met them with the statute book instead. It was not candlelight magic that broke the cars open, but paperwork, persistence, and the patience of someone who knew that delay is a trick as old as the gavel.

And yet to the city, this too became legend. When word spread that the court sided with her, that segregation was forced to crumble, the story swelled in retelling. "She bewitched the judges," some muttered. Others said she laid a curse on the companies, that she bent the steel tracks with her will. The truth was plainer, though no less powerful: she bent the law by wielding it.

To watch her in court was to learn that silence can be a weapon sharper than accusation. She listened more than she spoke, tilting her head just enough to make a witness falter. She allowed lawyers to bury themselves in arrogance, then tugged the rope of precedent until they found their footing gone. If a judge tried to bluster, she waited until the law itself whispered louder. She never needed to shout; the paper trail did it for her.

Outside the courtroom, streetcars clanged along their tracks as if nothing had changed. But for the riders who stepped aboard without being told to move, Pleasant's presence lingered in every ringing bell. She had forced a company, and through it, a city, to admit her humanity. That admission, once wrung out, could not be easily stuffed back into silence.

Still, the victories did not erase the battles elsewhere. In other courtrooms, she stood accused—by partners who betrayed her, by rivals who envied her, by heirs who clawed at her estate. There were lawsuits that dragged on for years, their language ugly with race and gender. She lost as often as she won. But even in defeat, she left a mark. Judges muttered that she was impossible to put down. Lawyers admitted, grudgingly, that she had a mind like a ledger.

To walk out of court, even with papers against her, was to remain in the city's mouth. They could not forget her, no matter how they tried.

In San Francisco, the courtroom was a stage, but the streetcar was a chorus. Every clang of its bell sang of Pleasant's legend: a woman who would not move when told, who turned humiliation into litigation, who understood that the law was a kind of spell if you spoke it often enough.

Thirty million was the rumor. Justice was the proof. Together they made her untouchable, if not always victorious. She became not only a figure of wealth and witchcraft but also of resistance carved into precedent. Her legend was no longer confined to parlors and alley whispers—it rattled along steel tracks, it echoed in law books, it clung to the city's daily rhythm.

And though rivals still spat her name in contempt, more than one passenger boarding a streetcar whispered it like a blessing.

Act VI

By the end of the century, the number had grown larger. Thirty million. It was painted across her life in brushstrokes wider than fact, thicker than ink. A figure that would not balance on ledgers, that would not reduce itself to neat columns, that drifted through San Francisco like a ghost coin.

The bankers said it with disbelief, as though spitting out a stone: *thirty million.* The gossiping ladies said it with relish, rolling it across their tongues like sugared almonds. The working men in saloons said it with awe, raising their glasses to the possibility that someone who looked like them might hold more gold than the city's crowned kings.

It became less a statement than a spell. The number itself was incantation. Whisper it, and she appeared—silks trailing, eyes sharp, smile thin. Whisper it, and a courtroom bent toward her. Whisper it, and fog seemed to draw tighter around Nob Hill's palaces, their granite faces uneasy.

It was like a monster growing out of control. Numbers have their own kind of existence. They live in rumor, in headlines, in fear. What mattered was that the city believed she *could*. That belief shaped her power as surely as any coin stacked in her desk.

She wore it not on her sleeve but in her bearing. A fortune that size, spoken into being, gave her the posture of inevitability. A woman worth thirty million could not be dismissed as a curiosity, could not be written off as a "Mammy" caricature. She was not a servant, not a novelty, not an aberration. She was a force, and the city could only explain her by inflating her into myth.

And Pleasant let them. She did not correct the number. She did not confirm it either. She allowed it to swell, to echo, to anchor itself in the fog. Thirty million became San Francisco's own chant, its own haunting, its own confession.

It is said that in her last years, when lawsuits had stripped her, when her name was dragged through courts and papers until her fortune dwindled, people still pointed to her and murmured: *that's the woman who was worth thirty million.* They said it at the market stalls, they said it outside her home, they said it long after her purse had grown thin. The number survived where the money did not.

That was her final victory. A rumor polished into legend, legend hardened into legacy. Thirty million as talisman, as shield, as weapon. Thirty million as the measure of a woman the city could not comprehend.

When she walked the streets of San Francisco in memory, even after her death, the fog carried it for her: **thirty million, thirty million, thirty million.**

And so the prologue closes, not on a balance sheet, but on an incantation. Before the story begins, before her railroads, before her courtroom wars, the reader is left with the truth that mattered most: that thirty million in current dollars would be easily one billion dollars: making Mary Ellen Pleasant a legend.

Part II

Black

Chapter 2

Birth of a Mogul

Act I

No one agrees where Mary Ellen Pleasant was born. That uncertainty became part of her legend, and she never rushed to cure it. Women who climb from the margins to mastery often emerge from contested openings; the fog that conceals their origins also protects their autonomy. Pleasant's first chapter sits between bondage and freedom, document and rumor - an ambiguity she learned to spend like coin.

One narrative places her birth on a Georgia plantation around 1814, where a child with skin "too light to be ignored and too dark to be spared" entered a world paced by overseers and ledgers. In that version she was born enslaved, a life measured

out in the arithmetic of cotton and compulsion.
The story functions as origin myth and analytic
key: if you start with chains, steel becomes habit.

Other tellings borrow Caribbean light. In these,
Pleasant's mother is a Haitian priestess and her
father a white official whose name conveniently
evaporates. The genealogy confers an aura that
later observers, uncomfortable with Black female
success in business, found easier to accept than
disciplined strategy. Sorcery, they implied, was
more plausible than spreadsheets.[1]

A different tradition claims Philadelphia. There,
among free Black families who lived in the legal
shallows between liberty and danger, a young girl
was apprenticed to a Quaker household, learned her
letters after work, and absorbed the quiet moral
stubbornness of Northern abolitionism. That origin comforts those who prefer a Northern arc of
uplift to a Southern crucible of survival.

Late in life Pleasant offered a version of her own.
Dictating to journalist Sam Davis in 1901, she
named Philadelphia as her birthplace, dated it August 19, 1814, identified her father as Louis Alexan-
der Williams, a silk merchant from the Sandwich
Islands (now Hawaii), and her mother as a free

---

[1]Lynn M. Hudson, *The Making of "Mammy Pleasant":
A Black Entrepreneur in Nineteenth-Century San Francisco*
(Urbana: University of Illinois Press, 2008), 17–20.

Black woman from Louisiana.[2] Whether this was
strict fact, strategic narrative, or both, she understood what modern biography confirms: the story
believed can shape the life adjudicated.

What the sources agree on is Nantucket. As a girl
or adolescent, Pleasant was placed with the Hussey
family - Quaker merchants whose parlors doubled
as abolitionist nodes. There she learned to read
and reckon, to keep tidy columns, to read a room
before she read a page. Quakers taught the uses of
silence, and Pleasant made silence a discipline. In
a world that would not hear a Black woman, she
developed the counter-skill of listening precisely
and remembering completely.[3]

Nantucket also offered an education in political
economy. Standing on the wharf, she watched
fortunes rise and vanish with the masts. The lesson
was blunt: wealth did not belong to the men who
rowed, hauled, and risked; it accrued to those
who owned the ships, controlled the insurance,
and wrote the contracts once the oil came ashore.
Labor made value; leverage captured it. Pleasant
kept that distinction.

By the time she left the island, Pleasant was less
a servant than a cipher: literate, numerate, observant, deliberately hard to pin down. And ciphers,

---

[2]Susheel Bibbs, *Her Name Was Mary Ellen Pleasant*
(San Francisco: MSS Press, 2019), 11.
[3]Hudson, *Making of "Mammy Pleasant"*, 23.

set against other people's ledgers, have a way of rearranging the sums.

Act II

San Francisco, the city that would later whisper and shout her name, had nothing to do with her beginning. Her first air belonged to another coast, and even there the archive speaks in fragments. To chase her childhood is to chase smoke; the effort still matters because of what the smoke reveals.

The Georgia account: bondage, scarcity, the iron curriculum of the plantation, explains her later endurance by rooting it in compulsion. The Philadelphia account - precarious freedom, Quaker rooms, apprenticeship, explains her later poise by rooting it in disciplined instruction. Both are plausible; both say as much about the tellers as they do about Pleasant. She allowed them to coexist because ambiguity, in a system eager to categorize, is a kind of freedom.

Nantucket is less ambiguous. Indenture arrangements placed Black and brown children inside white Quaker households as domestic laborers who were also, sometimes, students. In the Hussey home, household management was commerce by another name: provisioning, scheduling, accounting, reliability as a moral economy. Pleasant learned the vocabulary of receipts and the theology of punctuality. She also watched how influence circulates: how deference can be performed without surrender, how invisibility can be tactical rather than imposed.[4]

Silence in those rooms was not empty. It was an instrument. Pleasant learned when to remove herself, when to return, and how to make presence legible without speaking. Later, in California drawing rooms where money ate memory, she applied the same method: let others narrate; let their confidence expose assumptions; keep the account.

Even basic skills acquired there - clean longhand, double-entry habits, comfort around contracts, became structural advantages in a West where many men gambled with sums they could neither calculate nor sustain. The social technologies of a Quaker kitchen turned out to be the operating system of an urban frontier.

Questions remain about her status with the Husseys. Was she servant, foster child, paid apprentice, or a hybrid category the records do not neatly hold? The sources disagree, and Pleasant never corrected them. That, too, was a lesson: a past that cannot be fixed cannot be foreclosed.

If Georgia taught grit, Philadelphia taught caution, and a Haitian rumor taught useful mystique, Nan-

---

[4]For the blend of moral culture and maritime capitalism in Nantucket, see Christopher P. Magra, *Poseidon's Curse: British Naval Impressment and Atlantic Origins of the American Revolution* (New York: Cambridge University Press, 2016), 183–188; applied here as context.

tucket provided architecture – an internal ledger of how people, capital, and reputation move through systems. When she finally stepped into the boiling experiment of Gold Rush California, she did so with the patience of someone who had studied tides and the boldness of someone who could read a balance sheet.

Act III

By her early twenties, Pleasant had begun converting knowledge into motion. The Underground Railroad was a current without a cartographer, a network of parlors, kitchens, cellars, pulpits, docks. Quaker respectability supplied cover; Black communities supplied courage, information, and risk. The Railroad was, among other things, a logistics problem solved by trust.

In Boston, Pleasant married James Smith, a prosperous mulatto contractor and abolitionist. Their household combined capital with conviction. Money paid for food, shoes, and passage; discretion protected the people who provided them. Under the Fugitive Slave Act of 1850, every handshake risked prosecution. The law tried to nationalize bondage; the Railroad countered by nationalizing care.[5]

When Smith died, he left Pleasant more than funds.

---

[5]John Hope Franklin and Loren Schweninger, *Runaway Slaves: Rebels on the Plantation* (New York: Oxford University Press, 1999), 372.

He left a mandate to use resources with precision. Pleasant's philanthropy in this period is best
understood as infrastructure: financing couriers,
undergirding shelter, retaining counsel when counsel meant survival. Where others guided bodies
through forests, she moved money across jurisdic-
tions, and money, properly timed, is a kind of
vehicle.

Her name touches the orbit of John Brown. The
documentation is contested; the admiration is not.
Pleasant later called Brown "the bravest man
America ever produced" and said she aided him
"with my last dollar and my last prayer."[6] Whether
her dollars reached his palm matters less for biography than her public alignment after Harpers
Ferry. To claim Brown as martyr was to embrace
the argument that moral suasion alone could not
end a system built on stolen labor and legalized
violence. It was also to accept the costs of that
claim.

By the turn of the 1850s the nation's attention con-
vulsed westward. Gold exported men from households and prudence from ledgers. San Francisco
promised conversion, not of souls but of status.
Pleasant read the promise differently. She did not
intend to pan rivers; she intended to sell to the
men who did, invest in the routes they used, and
buy the ground they ignored.

---

[6]Hudson, *Making of "Mammy Pleasant"*, 41.

So she sailed, whether by Panama's fever path or the long arc around Cape Horn the sources do not agree, and reached San Francisco around 1852. The city she met was unripe and relentless: tents against dunes, timber against fog, gambling halls against hunger. It was a place where contracts could be drafted before breakfast and fortunes reversed by dusk. It was, in short, ideal terrain for someone who understood that the most durable gold rush is the one that flows through accounts rather than sluices.

In Georgia, they said she had been born in chains.
In Philadelphia, they said she had been born in freedom.
In New Orleans, they said she had been born of magic.
On Nantucket, they knew she had been born observant.

Yet to this country, she was a conductor of the Underground Railroad – a real American hero.

Chapter 3

John Brown:
Instrument of God

Act I – The Call

He was not born to moderation. From the pulpits of fiery abolitionists to the quiet ache of enslaved families fleeing north, John Brown heard a command that others dismissed as madness: God's demand for justice, swift and unrelenting. The Bible was his blueprint, the sword his punctuation.

Kansas bled, and Brown believed he had been summoned to stop the hemorrhage. His letters, full of Scripture and fury, spoke of covenant more than campaign. To him, slavery was not policy - it was sin. And sin could not be debated; it had to be slain. [1]

In that conviction, he resembled a prophet more than a politician. He gathered sons and strangers alike, shaping them into what he called the "Army of the Lord." His prayers were battle plans; his hymns, rehearsals for judgment.

Act II – The Fire in Kansas

They called it "Bleeding Kansas." Brown called it prophecy fulfilled. In May 1856, after pro-slavery raiders torched the free-state town of Lawrence, he answered not with rhetoric but retribution. At Pottawatomie Creek, he and his followers dragged five men from their cabins and executed them by night. [2]

News of the killings spread faster than the prairie wind. To his admirers, Brown had finally matched the nation's violence with its mirror image. To his enemies, he was a murderer cloaked in Scripture. Brown felt no need to defend himself. "I have no apology to make," he wrote; "it was necessary that this thing should be done." [3]

---

[1] David S. Reynolds, *John Brown, Abolitionist: The Man Who Killed Slavery, Sparked the Civil War, and Seeded Civil Rights* (New York: Vintage, 2005), 14–16.

[2] Louis A. DeCaro Jr., *Fire from the Midst of You: A Religious Life of John Brown* (New York: New York University Press, 2002), 180–182.

[3] John Brown, letter to his family, June 1856, in *The*

Kansas became his crucible. Amid burned farms and divided towns, he forged the theology that would define him: that the Republic's sin could not be purged except by blood. Years later, Lincoln would speak those same words, as if inheriting the echo.

—

Act III – The Siege at Harpers Ferry

In October 1859, John Brown descended upon Harpers Ferry, Virginia, with twenty-one men—black and white, free and formerly enslaved. Their aim was audacious: seize the federal armory, arm the enslaved, and ignite a revolution that would spread through the South like brushfire. [4]

The plan unraveled before dawn. Telegraph lines hummed faster than faith could travel. Marines under Colonel Robert E. Lee stormed the arsenal; Brown was struck down and captured, his sons dead beside him. When questioned, he spoke with calm defiance. "I deny everything but what I have all along admitted—the design on my part to free the slaves." [5]

Life and Letters of Captain John Brown, ed. Richard D. Webb (London: Sampson Low, 1861), 137.

[4]Tony Horwitz, *Midnight Rising: John Brown and the Raid That Sparked the Civil War* (New York: Henry Holt, 2011), 97–101.

[5]U.S. Senate, *Report of the Select Committee on the Harper's Ferry Invasion*, 36th Cong., 1st sess. (1860), 12.

For two days the nation argued his sanity. Ministers called him deluded; abolitionists called him saint. In his stillness, he seemed neither. Shackled and bleeding, he wrote that he was "quite certain that the crimes of this guilty land will never be purged away but with blood." [6]

Act IV – The Scaffold and the Seed

On December 2, 1859, John Brown walked to the gallows at Charlestown as if to an altar. The crowd came to see a spectacle; he offered them a sermon. His hands were bound, but his gaze was free. He looked out upon the hills and murmured, "This is a beautiful country." It was not beauty he meant—it was covenant. [7]

The trapdoor fell, and the stillness that followed was not silence but recoil. Bells tolled across the North; pulpits broke their restraint. Some called him murderer, others martyr, but none could deny that he had made the nation look directly at its own reflection—and flinch. [8]

---

[6] John Brown, "Last Letter to His Family," November 30, 1859, in *Life and Letters*, 355.

[7] David S. Reynolds, *John Brown, Abolitionist: The Man Who Killed Slavery, Sparked the Civil War, and Seeded Civil Rights* (New York: Vintage, 2005), 411–413.

[8] Tony Horwitz, *Midnight Rising: John Brown and the Raid That Sparked the Civil War* (New York: Henry Holt, 2011), 282–284.

Among those who watched the news spread westward was a woman whose name had already threaded through his cause. In Boston's hidden rooms, she had helped fund fugitives, fed conspiracies, and sent coin to those who carried Brown's letters. Mary Ellen Pleasant read of his death and whispered that she had "helped him with my last dollar and my last prayer." [9]

For her, Brown's hanging was not an ending but a signal. His body swung in Virginia; his shadow fell across the continent. She felt it in the tremor of every train wheel carrying settlers west, in every rumor of new fortunes and old injustices. If his sword had failed, her ledger would continue the war by other means. She would wield contracts where he had wielded steel, and in that discipline she would prove that resistance could be as shrewd as it was holy. [10]

When the newspapers laid his name to rest, hers began to travel. The Underground River that had once carried fugitives now flowed into a city of gold and fog. Out of the echo of his gallows, a new legend was already rising—one that would

---

[9]Mary Ellen Pleasant, interview by Sam Davis, 1901, in Lynn Hudson, *The Making of "Mammy Pleasant": A Black Entrepreneur in Nineteenth-Century San Francisco* (Urbana: University of Illinois Press, 2003), 47–48.

[10]Louis A. DeCaro Jr., *Fire from the Midst of You: A Religious Life of John Brown* (New York: NYU Press, 2002), 316.

walk the streets of San Francisco in silks, balance ledgers like psalms, and bend the law as deftly as Brown had bent Scripture.

The fire did not die at Harpers Ferry. It crossed the continent, wearing another name.

Chapter 4

The Underground River

Act I

The river was always moving, though no map recorded it. It flowed beneath the soil of the republic, carried in whispers and lantern signals, in doors left unlatched and wagons rolling after midnight. Its waters were made of courage and silence, of hands passing fugitives along like driftwood toward the sea. And Mary Ellen Pleasant knew its current.

No one knows when she first stepped into that secret tide. Perhaps it was in Nantucket, where Quaker households argued abolition over tea while she listened from the corner, her silence sharper than their rhetoric.   Perhaps it was in Boston, where her marriage to James Smith, a wealthy mulatto contractor, gave her both protection and coin. Or perhaps she was already a conductor long before, instinctively opening her doors, carrying messages in her eyes, moving like the river itself, unseen, unstoppable.

The stories that survive read like parables.   A knock at midnight, answered by a young woman with steady hands.   A fugitive hidden beneath laundry in a cart bound for the next town. Coins slipped across a table, enough for passage north, never recorded in any ledger. A prayer whispered not for salvation but for silence, because silence could save lives more reliably than sermons.

And always, Pleasant's presence at the edge of the tale: arranging, directing, watching. She did not seek the role of heroine. She preferred to be the shadow in the corridor, the seamstress whose stitches no one noticed until the fabric held.

Some whispered that she met with Frederick Douglass himself, though no record confirms it. What we do know, is that she provided financing for John Brown, helping to feed the fire that would blaze at Harpers Ferry. What cannot be denied is that she later claimed him as a friend, even a martyr, and spoke of him with reverence long after the gallows silenced him. She sent valuable dollars to help abolitionist efforts, In the same way, that John Hancock helped to finance the American Revolution.

The river had many faces. For the fugitives, it was salvation. For the conductors, it was duty. For Pleasant, it was apprenticeship in power. She learned that money was not just survival, it was leverage. A few coins at the right moment could mean life. A trusted word could turn a law into dust. A connection, once made, could ripple outward like circles in water.

Act II

Her path through the Underground River was not walked alone. In Boston she met **James Smith**, a wealthy mulatto contractor, older than her, already established. He had money earned from contracts and careful business, and he had convictions. He believed in abolition, not only as sentiment but as action.

Boston was alive with abolitionist energy, and Pleasant moved through its circles like a thread stitching hidden seams. Quaker parlors, Black churches, merchants' offices; all became stations in the greater network. She listened more than she spoke. Her silences unnerved some, impressed others. In her presence, people felt their secrets weighed, their intentions measured.

She saw how reputations could be leveraged. How alliances could be forged across unlikely lines: white

Quakers and Black entrepreneurs, fiery preachers
and quiet conductors. She learned to map influence
as carefully as any cartographer mapped rivers. A
single letter of introduction could move a fugitive
further than a wagon; a single contact in the right
office could erase the trail of a bounty hunter.

Mary and her husband bent their lives toward
abolition. The city hummed with the voice of
William Lloyd Garrison, his *Liberator* carrying
words as sharp as blades, and her new husband
lent his own pen to its cause. Together they opened
their doors to fugitives, guiding men and women
north into Canada and south into Mexico, through
the hidden lattice of homes and hands that made
up the Underground Railroad.

James Smith passed away. Their marriage was less
romance than alliance, though some say there was
affection, perhaps even devotion. What mattered
most was partnership. Smith trusted her with his
affairs. He encouraged her to act boldly in the
cause of freedom. Some claim that when he died,
he left her not only an inheritance but a mission:
use it well, use it for our people.

Money became her secret weapon on the Railroad.
While others risked their lives guiding fugitives
across fields and forests, she often moved the river
with silver and gold. Food, clothing, train tickets,
legal aid—these things required funds. Pleasant
was a conductor not just of fugitives but of re-

sources. She could turn money into motion, and motion into salvation.

With that money she pushed further into the struggle, alone for a time, and then with John Pleasants at her side, a former employee who became her husband. His name drifted in the records: Plaissance, Pleasance, but Mary Ellen made it simple: Pleasant.

Her work grew heavier, more visible, and with it came danger. Slave catchers took notice. Their eyes turned toward her, their hands itched for reward. To escape the tightening noose, she fled south to New Orleans with John. Yet even there the shadow of pursuit lengthened, and so she looked farther still westward. To California. From that moment on, John Pleasants faded into silence, while Mary carried the name, the fire, and the fight forward alone.

It was here she discovered her greatest strength: the ability to move unseen, to finance freedom without leaving fingerprints.

Later, when San Francisco's barons whispered that she was omnipresent, they did not realize she had been trained in omnipresence years earlier, in Boston's abolitionist dens.

Act III

And then came John Brown. His name thundered through abolitionist circles long before Harpers

Ferry, carried not just in newspapers but in whispers traded at meetings, in letters passed from hand to hand, in sermons that never dared say his name but still set pulpits aflame with his spirit. To his friends, he was a man of granite faith and violent mercy; to his enemies, he was a fanatic with blood on his hands. To Pleasant, whether she met him or only brushed the edges of his orbit, he was something more, a symbol, an omen, a test of what freedom truly demanded.

He was fire where others were water, uncompromising, fierce, convinced that freedom must be taken by steel if not by word. While Frederick Douglass sharpened speeches, Brown sharpened blades. While William Lloyd Garrison laid out columns of careful argument, Brown studied maps, plotted raids, and whispered of insurrection in taverns and boarding houses. Pleasant understood both sides of that coin: the necessity of rhetoric and the inevitability of violence. She had built her life on persuasion, cunning, and careful maneuver, yet she knew: as any enslaved woman knew, that the lash did not yield to reason, that iron chains did not fall away through polite conversation. Brown gave voice to that truth, loud and merciless, and she felt its echo.

Some say Pleasant met him, eye to eye, in those restless Boston years when she was gathering funds, information, and allies in the city's abolitionist salons. Perhaps their gazes locked across a crowded

hall, his eyes burning with prophecy, hers calcu-
lating, steady, appraising whether his fire could
be bent toward her own designs. Others say she
only sent him money; discreet, untraceable sums
slipped into the abolitionist networks that stitched
the North together. Quiet support that vanished
into the furnace of his plans, as good money always
did.

Later, when asked, she did not hedge. She claimed
him as comrade and martyr. "He died for the
cause," she said without hesitation, as if his blood
had written her own creed.   She spoke of him
with a reverence that scandalized San Francisco
decades later, where respectable society wanted to
tidy the past, to file Brown away as a lunatic, an
aberration. Pleasant refused. She kept his memory
raw, unsanitized, insisting that his gallows was as
holy as any altar.

Whether or not she placed dollars into his palm,
she placed her name beside his, and that was dangerous enough.   To align with Brown was not
merely to call slavery unjust; it was to declare
it an enemy that could not be bargained with,
that had to be broken, shattered like a chain on
an anvil. It meant you did not flinch at the word
"rebellion," that you recognized blood as the price
already paid by the enslaved, and thus a price the
enslavers might one day have to pay in return.

Pleasant carried that conviction westward like a

hidden brand, one she would never entirely put down. In California, she played the role of entrepreneur, benefactor, even mythmaker, but beneath the silks and strategies smoldered that ember lit by Brown's raid. His failure at Harpers Ferry did not extinguish it—it burned more fiercely, proof that even a doomed strike could sear the conscience of a nation. Wherever Pleasant moved, whispers followed: that she had funded Brown, that she had known him, that she had dreamed his same impossible dream. She did not rush to deny it. The legend suited her, even when it endangered her, because the truth was simpler and harder: she believed as he believed. Slavery was not to be argued with. It was to be ended—by word if possible, by steel if required.

Chapter 5

The Fever Called Gold

History has its earthquakes. Some split nations; others shake the ground beneath ordinary people and scatter them across the world. In 1848, one such tremor began not with cannon or crown but with the strike of a shovel at a sawmill beside the American River. A few bright flakes glittered in the tailrace—dust no bigger than a fingernail—and the modern world changed course. [1]

Act I – Rumor

When James Marshall carried those flakes to John

---

[1] H. W. Brands, *The Age of Gold: The California Gold Rush and the New American Dream* (New York: Anchor Books, 2003), 1–5.

Sutter, the Swiss immigrant who owned the mill, both men swore secrecy. They had reason. Sutter's empire—fields, livestock, vineyards—depended on discipline, not frenzy. But in a territory where gossip traveled faster than the mail, silence was impossible. Within weeks, soldiers returning from the Mexican–American War carried whispers east: "Gold in California." [2]

By December, President James K. Polk confirmed it before Congress. The remark was almost off-hand—a paragraph in a long address—but the effect was seismic. Newspapers reprinted the speech as revelation; preachers folded it into sermons; merchants stamped it on crates. By the spring of 1849, ports from Boston to Valparaíso had emptied. Ships sold their cargoes for shovels and left their crews behind. California became less a destination than an idea.

The movement had no precedent. Tens of thousands abandoned farms, shops, and families, convinced that providence had shifted west. A minister in Missouri called it "a second Exodus." A sailor in Sydney wrote home that he had seen "men mad with sunlight." The name "Forty-Niner" would come to dignify them, but at the time they were simply migrants in a trance.

---

[2]Kevin Starr, *Americans and the California Dream, 1850–1915* (New York: Oxford University Press, 1973), 12–16.

Act II – Conquest Recast

The gold rush began in a vacuum of government. Only months earlier, Mexico had surrendered the province to the United States. The Treaty of Guadalupe Hidalgo promised citizenship to the region's Mexican residents and protection to its Indigenous peoples; both promises dissolved on contact with gold. Military rule gave way to improvisation—vigilance committees, miners' codes, rough elections held in saloons. Law was whatever fifty armed men would sign. [3]

The cost to Native California was immediate and catastrophic. Before 1848, the Indigenous population numbered perhaps 150,000; within a generation, fewer than 30,000 survived. Vigilante expeditions—subsidized by local governments—hunted entire villages under the pretext of retrieving stolen stock. Kidnapping and forced labor reappeared under new euphemisms such as "apprenticeship" or "indenture." In this sense, California entered the Union baptized not only in gold but in blood.
[4]

Act III – The City on the Bay

San Francisco, a sleepy village of adobe houses and

[3]Robert W. Cherny, *California: A History* (Hoboken: Wiley-Blackwell, 2011), 43–45.

[4]Benjamin Madley, *An American Genocide: The United States and the California Indian Catastrophe, 1846–1873* (New Haven: Yale University Press, 2016), 107–112.

abandoned ships, became the rush's laboratory. In 1847 it held fewer than a thousand residents; by 1852, more than thirty-six thousand. A forest of masts filled the harbor, each vessel turned into warehouse or tavern. Streets of planked pine sank under mud; canvas roofs flapped in the sea wind like banners of temporary republics. The air reeked of salt, gunpowder, and speculation. [5]

Here was capitalism in its rawest form—unregulated, unrepentant, magnificent. Banks appeared overnight and collapsed by dawn. Fires devoured whole blocks only to be followed by grander reconstructions. The gambling dens operated as informal stock exchanges; the wharves doubled as courts of arbitration. The city minted its own currency when Washington's coinage failed to arrive. It was said a man could walk down Montgomery Street with a handful of nuggets and return that evening ruined or reborn.

Among the early fortunes were names that would later decorate universities and railroads: Stanford, Crocker, Huntington. None of them dug for ore. They sold tools, transport, and vision. The lesson was simple and enduring—control the infrastructure, not the dream. The gold was finite; ambition was not. [6]

---

[5]Malcolm J. Rohrbough, *Days of Gold: The California Gold Rush and the American Nation* (Berkeley: University of California Press, 1997), 89–94.

[6]Starr, *Americans and the California Dream*, 22–24.

Act IV – Babel

The miners' camps became Babels of language and grievance. Chinese laborers chanted work songs beside Irish immigrants; Mexican vaqueros showed New Englanders how to pan. Yet the ideal of equality cracked quickly. The first legislature of the new state, admitted to the Union in 1850, imposed a foreign miners' tax and barred nonwhites from testifying against whites in court. What had begun as a democratic fever hardened into a hierarchy of color. [7]

Chinese miners, who by 1852 numbered more than 20,000, faced mob expulsions from the diggings; Latin American workers were beaten and deported; African Americans, though few, were forced to purchase "freedom certificates" to avoid enslavement under local law. The Gold Rush made California wealthy and unequal in the same stroke—a dual inheritance it would never entirely shed. [8]

Act V – The Mechanics of Extraction

At first, prospectors worked alone, crouched over pans and rockers. Within three years, industrial

---

[7]Stacey L. Smith, *Freedom's Frontier: California and the Struggle over Unfree Labor, Emancipation, and Reconstruction* (Chapel Hill: University of North Carolina Press, 2013), 23–27.

[8]Jean Pfaelzer, *Driven Out: The Forgotten War Against Chinese Americans* (New York: Random House, 2007), 45–50.

method replaced hope. Sluice boxes stretched for miles; water wheels powered pumps; then came hydraulic mining—cannons of water that could strip entire hillsides to bedrock. Rivers turned the color of mercury. Forests vanished into flumes. The Sacramento Valley began to flood under tons of displaced silt. [9]

The miners themselves became wage laborers in corporations funded by Eastern capital. A frontier once imagined as the last sanctuary of independence was recast as an open-air factory. The West, long mythologized as freedom's horizon, became the proving ground for industrial America.

Act VI – The Lives Behind the Ledgers

Women's presence—statistically negligible, culturally decisive—reshaped the boomtowns. For every twenty men, there was one woman, and scarcity conferred both peril and power. Some cooked, washed, and kept boardinghouses; others performed on rough stages or managed brothels that doubled as banks. Domestic labor itself became a form of speculation. [10]

African American pioneers, though small in number, carried abolitionist energy westward. Newspa-

---

[9] Andrew C. Isenberg, *Mining California: An Ecological History* (New York: Hill and Wang, 2005), 58–63.

[10] JoAnn Levy, *They Saw the Elephant: Women in the California Gold Rush* (Norman: University of Oklahoma Press, 1992), 33–37.

pers such as *The Elevator* and *The Pacific Appeal* would later grow from this community. Free Black settlers founded churches, schools, and mutual-aid societies, asserting civic presence in a state that denied them citizenship. The contradiction was stark: a free state that mimicked slave codes. [11]

Act VII – The Moral Arithmetic

By 1855, the easy gold was gone. A million souls had come through California's ports, and most left poorer than they arrived. Yet the myth endured—that a single discovery could overturn the order of the world. It became the secular gospel of the age: salvation through risk. Gold replaced grace; speculation replaced faith. The nation, newly rich and restless, began to imagine success as proof of virtue.

In this climate, character itself was measured like ore—by yield. Those who could turn chaos into stability were the new prophets. A merchant who sold shovels wisely, a banker who lent at the right hour, a woman who understood the arithmetic of hunger and ambition—all were participants in a second creation story, one written in ledgers instead of scripture.

Act VIII – The Arrival

It was into this laboratory of greed and reinvention

---

[11]Delilah L. Beasley, *The Negro Trail Blazers of California* (Los Angeles: Times-Mirror, 1919), 14–18.

that Mary Ellen Pleasant arrived. The ships still crowded the bay, their hulls creaking under layers of fog. On the hills, mansions began to sprout beside shanties. The language of speculation was everywhere: shares, lots, ventures, stakes. In this cacophony, a woman trained in silence found advantage.

She did not come to mine but to measure, not to dig but to deal. Where others saw a river glittering with chance, she saw an economy desperate for order. Behind her lay the Underground Railroad and the martyrdom of John Brown; ahead, a city that worshiped profit but distrusted the hands that made it. California, reborn by gold, was ready for a different kind of alchemy.

The fever had spent itself, yet its heat remained—in the soil, in the markets, in the dreams of those who believed fortune could be summoned by will. Out of that lingering fire, she would shape her own legend.

Chapter 6

The Circles Around Mary Ellen

After the Rush

When the fever of gold cooled, California hardened into capital. By the early 1850s, the same streets that once echoed with miners' shouts were lined with countinghouses, legal offices, and warehouses of imported grain. Wealth no longer came from rivers; it came from contracts. The people who thrived were not prospectors but negotiators—those who could convert fortune into structure, chance into credit.

Mary Ellen Pleasant entered that world at precisely the moment when improvisation was giving way

to institutions. The United States Mint opened
a branch in San Francisco in 1854, stabilizing the
region's chaotic currency; private banks formed
syndicates to fund infrastructure and rail. The
Civil War, though fought far to the east, acceler-
ated California's transformation from frontier to
financial satellite of the Union. Into this new economy stepped Pleasant—experienced in discretion,
fluent in both Black abolitionist circles and the
language of business risk.

For a woman of color to own property was nearly
impossible under California's 1850 constitution,
which restricted citizenship and legal testimony
to white men. Yet Pleasant would come to hold,
through proxies, an estate valued in the millions.
Her genius was relational. To understand her story
is to map the people who made it possible—or tried
to destroy it.

Economic Circles: The Archi-
tecture of Trust

Thomas Bell: The Partner Behind
the Deeds

Among the earliest surviving records linking Pleasant to wealth are property deeds filed in San Francisco County between 1866 and 1877 under the

name of Thomas Bell, a Scottish-born banker and investor in mining and transportation stocks. Bell, who had arrived in California during the early 1850s, was a founding director of the Bank of California and a partner in the firm Bell, Ralston & Company. Archival evidence shows that numerous properties attributed to him were in fact financed by Pleasant's capital, often derived from her lucrative network of boardinghouses and catering contracts. [1]

Bell and Pleasant's relationship defied the racial and gender hierarchies of nineteenth-century San Francisco. She was a free Black woman in her forties; he, a white man of comfortable means and social standing. Their partnership was both pragmatic and subversive. Under California law, Pleasant could not testify in court or enter most contracts in her own name. Bell served as legal façade for her ventures, signing deeds and loan instruments while Pleasant managed the businesses and finances. The arrangement was mutually beneficial: Bell gained access to her capital and managerial skill; she gained legitimacy in the eyes of the banking establishment.

Rumor, inevitably, transformed business into scandal. Newspapers insinuated impropriety, calling

---

[1]Lynn M. Hudson, *The Making of "Mammy Pleasant"* (Urbana: University of Illinois Press, 2003), 53–59; San Francisco County Deed Book, vol. 42 (1868), 112–115.

Pleasant "the shadow of Nob Hill," a figure who haunted the periphery of respectability. Yet Bell's own ledgers—discovered after his death in 1892—record loans and dividends traceable to Pleasant's accounts, confirming her status as investor rather than dependent. [2]

Teresa Bell: Widow, Adversary, Historian

If Thomas Bell's records prove Pleasant's economic power, his widow Teresa's lawsuits preserve the social backlash it provoked. Teresa Bell, twenty years her husband's junior, filed multiple suits between 1877 and 1897 seeking to reclaim property and damages from Pleasant. The filings accuse Pleasant of "undue influence," "domination," and "hypnotic control"—language that reveals as much about race and gender anxiety as about finance. [3]

Teresa's testimony, serialized in the *San Francisco Chronicle*, casts Pleasant as an "enchantress of dusky hue" who had "mesmerized a man of business." The court, while skeptical of such imagery, nonetheless voided several property transfers, stripping Pleasant of holdings she had financed. Her

---

[2]Hudson, *Mammy Pleasant*, 95–97; San Francisco Probate File #18422, Estate of Thomas Bell (1892).

[3]Teresa Bell, *Complaint in Bell v. Pleasant*, San Francisco Superior Court, 1877, Bell Estate Case Files.

defeat was procedural, not moral; without the ability to testify fully or present her own accounts as
evidence, she was legally invisible in a courtroom
that consumed her reputation for spectacle.

These proceedings reveal a crucial truth about
Pleasant's world: economic power was inseparable
from racialized performance. To defend her investments, she had to inhabit two personas—the silent
capitalist behind Bell's signature, and the public
"Mammy Pleasant" invented by hostile journalists.
In both guises, she remained an anomaly: a Black
woman whose wealth required white witnesses to
exist.

Networks of Credit and Color

Pleasant's partnership with Bell was not an iso-
lated act but part of a larger pattern of cross-racial
financial cooperation in post–Gold Rush California.
City directories and tax ledgers from the 1860s list
numerous "colored boardinghouses" that catered
to transient workers and miners; several, according to the *Daily Alta California*, were "under the
efficient management of a Mrs. Pleasant." [4]

She extended microloans to laundresses, cooks,
and small merchants—largely women—operating
on the margins of legitimacy. Though her meth-

---

[4] *Daily Alta California*, February 14, 1863, 4.

ods resembled those of a banker, her motive was partly communal: she financed livelihoods denied conventional credit. These informal economies, mostly unrecorded, formed the economic spine of San Francisco's Black population before Reconstruction.

Her banking arrangements brought her into contact with figures like William C. Ralston, founder of the Bank of California, and D. O. Mills, another financier of the era. Surviving ledgers in the Bank's archive list deposits under Thomas Bell's name corresponding to Pleasant's known ventures, indicating she operated within the same circuits of capital as the city's elite. [5]

Through these networks, Pleasant became an unseen architect of San Francisco's growth. The Bell mansion on Octavia Street, often described as her residence though legally Bell's, was both office and refuge—a site where business meetings and community gatherings intertwined. To the city's powerful, it was an anomaly; to the dispossessed, it was proof that wealth could wear a Black face.

---

[5]Bank of California Archives, Ledger C, 1867–1869, entries 197–201.

Economic Context and Consequence

Pleasant's ascent occurred during a period of volatile speculation. The Comstock Lode silver boom of the 1860s and the Panic of 1873 reshaped California's financial landscape. Her diversification into real estate, service industries, and transportation buffered her against collapse. By 1870, according to tax assessments, she controlled holdings valued at approximately $150,000 (equivalent to about $4 million today). [6]

Her wealth, however, was structurally precarious—secured by relationships rather than title. When Bell died and Teresa Bell challenged ownership, Pleasant's fortune unraveled. Yet even in decline she left traces in corporate registries and court transcripts, showing a woman who mastered credit economies decades before women could open bank accounts independently.

In the architecture of nineteenth-century trust, Pleasant built her own foundation out of social contradiction. Her capital was belief: belief in her discretion, her reliability, her capacity to move between worlds. Those who partnered with her—Bell, Ralston, the restaurateurs and merchants whose names filled her ledgers—found profit in that belief. Those who opposed her found that the same

---

[6]San Francisco Tax Assessor's Records, 1870, Ward 6, entries 412–415.

invisibility which made her powerful also made her
defenseless.

Legal Circles: Law as Terrain

In nineteenth-century California, law was both
obstacle and instrument. The state's founding
constitution of 1850 barred people of African or
Native descent from testifying against whites; its
courts were saturated with the logic of exclusion
even as the Gold Rush demanded order. Within
that contradiction, Mary Ellen Pleasant learned
to wield procedure itself as leverage. She appeared in records not as a supplicant but as a
litigant—sometimes plaintiff, sometimes defendant,
always strategist.

Civil Rights in the Streetcar Era

The first of Pleasant's known legal actions, *Pleasant v. North Beach & Mission Railroad Co.* (1866),
began with a simple refusal. One afternoon she
boarded a horse-drawn streetcar and was ordered
off because of her race. She resisted, citing her
fare and dignity as equal currency. The conductor
ejected her forcibly. Two years later, after similar
incidents, she financed a parallel suit, *Pleasant
v. Omnibus Co.* Together, the cases forced the
question of public accommodation before San Francisco's bench. [7]

---

[7]William C. Beecher, "Mary Ellen Pleasant and the California Streetcar Cases," *California Legal History* 7 (2012):

Judge William T. Wallace ruled that a private
carrier licensed by the city performed a public
function and therefore could not arbitrarily exclude
passengers. While his opinion stopped short of a
sweeping desegregation mandate, it affirmed that
citizenship implied the right of transit. When
the California legislature codified that principle
in 1868, Pleasant's suits became the uncredited
precedent behind it. [8]

Pleasant never styled herself as a reformer. She
used litigation as protection for her class mobil-
ity: she refused to be denied access to the same
streetcars that carried her white business partners.
Yet the consequences rippled outward. By 1872
San Francisco's Black residents could point to her
victories as early civil-rights law—nearly a century
before the federal Civil Rights Act of 1964.

The Courtroom as Stage

Courtrooms in Gilded-Age San Francisco doubled
as theatre. Reporters from the *Daily Alta California* and *San Francisco Chronicle* filled their
columns with sketches of litigants and whispered
intrigue from counsel tables. Pleasant understood

121–133.

    [8]Kevin Starr, *Americans and the California Dream,
1850–1915* (New York: Oxford University Press, 1973),
60–62.

this dynamic intuitively. When summoned, she appeared in sober dress, rarely speaking, letting her lawyers argue technicalities while her silence drew attention.

Her streetcar cases attracted abolitionist observers; later, her property suits drew speculators and gossip-seekers. In both, she demonstrated mastery of image. The racist press caricatured her as "Mammy Pleasant," a figure of superstition; she weaponized the caricature, using its supposed harmlessness as cover for shrewd negotiation. In the archive she exists at once as stereotype and tactician—a paradox sustained by her own performance.

The Bell Estate Litigation

After Thomas Bell's accidental death in 1892, Pleasant became entangled in a decade of probate proceedings that exposed the machinery of wealth and prejudice in late-nineteenth-century California. Teresa Bell filed claims alleging that Pleasant had "exercised dominion" over her husband through "mesmeric powers." The accusations blurred legal argument with spiritual panic, portraying interracial business partnership as moral corruption. [9]

---

[9]Teresa Bell, *Complaint in Bell v. Pleasant*, San Francisco Superior Court, 1877, Bell Estate Case Files.

Judge Samuel Buckley dismissed the charges of
witchcraft but ordered financial audits that effec-
tively dismantled Pleasant's holdings. Lacking for-
mal title to most properties, she could claim ownership only through correspondence and witness
testimony—forms of evidence discounted when offered by Black litigants. The trials consumed years
and eroded her remaining fortune. Yet within
the transcripts survive glimpses of her financial
acuity: itemized rents, loan ledgers, and cross-
examinations in which she corrected opposing counsel's arithmetic. [10]

The estate suits illuminate how California law
functioned as a sieve through which race, gender,
and class were filtered. Property could pass only
through white hands; testimony gained weight according to the speaker's color. Pleasant's downfall,
in legal terms, was procedural. The same system
that had recognized her right to a streetcar seat
refused to recognize her right to a deed.

Legal Culture and Strategy

Pleasant's repeated resort to litigation places her
within a broader continuum of nineteenth-century
African American legal activism. Across the country, Black plaintiffs used state courts to challenge

---

[10]Hudson, *The Making of "Mammy Pleasant"* (Urbana:
University of Illinois Press, 2003), 95–102.

exclusion even before federal Reconstruction. What distinguishes Pleasant is scale: her cases dealt not merely with access but with ownership.

Her attorneys—often white men from the commercial bar—treated her both as client and curiosity. Surviving correspondence between her lawyer Thomas Fitch and city attorney Henry Haight reveals a grudging respect for her intelligence. Fitch wrote in 1878 that "the woman Pleasant knows every figure in her accounts better than any man in my office." [11]

These exchanges show how she transformed the courtroom into an extension of her business life: adversarial, calculated, and always public. For Pleasant, litigation was not deviation but continuation—another mode of negotiation when ordinary contract was denied her.

Judges and Precedent

The judges who presided over her cases—Wallace, Sawyer, Buckley—belonged to a generation struggling to reconcile frontier informality with codified justice. Their opinions on Pleasant, scattered across reporters' notes and minute books, chart the slow domestication of California law from im-

---

[11]Thomas Fitch to Henry Haight, October 3, 1878, California State Library, Manuscripts Division.

provisation to bureaucracy. Wallace's 1866 opinion cited natural-law equality; Buckley's 1890s decisions invoked property codes and fiduciary duty. The shift mirrors the narrowing of the American moral imagination after Reconstruction: equality gave way to order.

By engaging the courts for half a century, Pleasant became an unwitting chronicler of that transition. The law changed around her—from a tool she could bend to a cage she could not escape. Yet each case left sediment: citations later used in civil-rights arguments, financial precedents quietly acknowledging her competence, and a record proving that legal exclusion could still produce legal legacy.

Political Circles: The Black Community and the Abolitionist Network

Pleasant's business acumen gave her independence; her politics gave it meaning. She arrived in California at a time when African Americans numbered fewer than two thousand in a population exceeding 380,000. Dispersed and disfranchised, they nevertheless built churches, newspapers, and conventions that made San Francisco the nerve center of Black civic life on the Pacific coast. Pleasant's presence within this network is documented not through self-promotion but through receipts, donations, and the ink of others.

Community Institutions and Clergy

By 1858 San Francisco's African Methodist Episcopal Zion and First African Methodist Episcopal congregations had become the primary organizing spaces for political discourse. Pleasant appears in early membership rolls as "contributor" rather than communicant—a distinction that reflects both her unconventional piety and her material leverage. [12]

---

[12]Delilah L. Beasley, *The Negro Trail Blazers of California* (Los Angeles: Times-Mirror, 1919), 55–58.

Reverend James R. Hardenbergh, an outspoken abolitionist preacher, recorded in an 1865 church report that "Mrs. M. E. Pleasant has rendered aid to the brethren without asking name or favor." [13] Her donations underwrote rent, travel for delegates to state colored conventions, and legal fees for those contesting racially restrictive ordinances. These gifts were strategic: they reinforced institutions capable of collective bargaining at a time when individual protest invited retaliation.

The Colored Conventions Movement

California's "Colored Citizens' Conventions," beginning in 1855, sought to secure testimony rights, suffrage, and access to education. Pleasant never appeared among elected officers, yet the convention minutes often note her name in subscription lists and hospitality acknowledgments. In 1857, delegates meeting at Bethel AME Zion recorded "thanks to Mrs. M. E. Pleasant for entertainment and contribution of $50 toward expenses." [14]

That amount, modest today, equaled nearly two months' wages for a skilled laborer. Through such quiet patronage she exercised influence without exposure. Her pattern was consistent: fund the

[13]Hardenbergh Report, AME Archives, 1865.

[14]Minutes of the California State Convention of Colored Citizens, Sacramento, 1857, California State Library.

movement, avoid the microphone. To many male
leaders trained in oratory, this discretion read as
aloofness; in hindsight it appears as tactical invisibility.

Abolitionist Correspondence and National Ties

Before her westward move, Pleasant had lived in
Boston, working among the interracial abolitionist networks surrounding Lewis Tappan, Wendell
Phillips, and George L. Stearns—the latter a prin-
cipal backer of John Brown's raid at Harpers Ferry.
While no surviving letters between Pleasant and
Brown exist, an 1860 note from Stearns to fellow
abolitionist Thomas Wentworth Higginson men-
tions "our colored friend M.E.P. now at the Pacific,
still faithful and useful." [15]

Pleasant later claimed in interviews that she had
"helped Brown with my last dollar and my last
prayer." Whether literal or symbolic, the statement
fits the financial pattern of Boston's Black abolitionist women—figures such as Ellen Craft and
Harriet Jacobs—whose contributions rarely survived in ledgers but whose networks kept fugitives
fed and armed. Her gravestone's epitaph, "She
was a friend of John Brown," converts memory

---

[15]George L. Stearns to Thomas Wentworth Higginson,
April 12, 1860, Massachusetts Historical Society.

into creed.

Reconstruction on the Pacific

After the Civil War, California did not experience
Reconstruction in law, but its Black residents at-
tempted it in practice. They petitioned for the
repeal of testimony bans, the establishment of
equal schooling, and the protection of labor contracts. Pleasant's funds appeared again—this time
in support of the *Pacific Appeal* newspaper and its
successor, *The Elevator*, edited by Peter Anderson
and Philip A. Bell. Their columns documented everything from voting rights petitions to the moral
dangers of "color prejudice imported from the Atlantic." [16]

Bell referred to Pleasant in 1868 as "our good sister
whose hand is always open to the race." Anderson, more cautious, described her as "of independent means and independent spirit." The newspapers' gratitude also signaled tension: Pleasant's
independence exceeded the gender expectations of
her peers. In a community seeking respectability
through temperance and religious conformity, her
rumored wealth and cosmopolitan manners were
both inspiration and scandal.

---

[16]*Pacific Appeal*, March 10, 1866, 2; *The Elevator*, July
12, 1867, 3.

Race, Gender, and Class Politics

Pleasant's political significance lies in her synthe-
sis of three identities rarely aligned in the 1860s
West—Black, female, and capitalist. While male
contemporaries such as Peter Lester and Mifflin
Gibbs pursued respectability through small business and civic petition, she wielded investment
as protest. Her ownership of property in a city
that denied her personhood constituted an act of
resistance more radical than many speeches.

Local authorities read her success as threat. The
1866 tax rolls record higher assessments for her
properties than comparable white-owned boardinghouses—a pattern mirrored across California
when Black prosperity challenged fiscal hierarchies.
By insisting on paying taxes in her own name,
she claimed the political identity those taxes were
meant to fund: citizenship.

Legacy of the Political Circle

By the 1880s the Black population of San Francisco
had stabilized around 1,800, dwarfed by Chinese
and European immigrant communities. Yet its
institutions endured—churches, mutual-aid societies, and the press—each owing something to
Pleasant's earlier patronage. Her political method
anticipated later Black women's activism in the

Progressive Era: financing suits, mentoring youth, and using domestic economies as seed capital for public justice.

Her role in the abolitionist network thus forms one continuous arc—from Boston's fugitive corridors to San Francisco's boardrooms. She embodied the transition from the moral economy of emancipation to the capitalist pragmatism of Reconstruction. Through money, she practiced politics; through discretion, she preserved survival.

Public Circles: Reputation, Journalism, and Mythmaking

By the 1870s Mary Ellen Pleasant's name had moved from ledgers to headlines. The city that once needed her capital now fed on her legend. In San Francisco's newspapers she became, by turns, a sorceress, a philanthropist, a blackmailer, and an oracle of finance. Her reputation was less biography than public negotiation—a dialogue between a woman who refused transparency and a society that could not imagine her power without magic.

The Press and the Making of "Mammy Pleasant"

The earliest printed use of the term "Mammy Pleasant" appears in the *San Francisco Chronicle* of April 1877, describing her as "the colored confidante of Nob Hill's elite." The label echoed the post-Civil War plantation stereotype of the loyal nursemaid, repurposed to domesticate her threat. [17] By calling a financier "Mammy," the white press reduced entrepreneurial genius to household service. The nickname stuck because it flattered prejudice: it allowed the city to marvel at her

---

[17]Lynn M. Hudson, *The Making of "Mammy Pleasant"* (Urbana: University of Illinois Press, 2003), 83–85.

wealth while denying her authority.

Pleasant rarely corrected the record. She signed no public letters, issued no manifestos. Silence became her editorial policy—a calculated refusal that let rumor circulate without contradiction. To some readers, that silence confirmed guilt; to others, it suggested discipline. The press, lacking direct access, filled the void with invention. Stories of séances, voodoo altars, and hidden gold circulated through papers from San Francisco to New York, each borrowing from the gothic language used for women who owned too much.

Gender, Race, and the Gaze of Sensation

The Gilded Age press thrived on scandal. Wealthy women were spectacle; wealthy Black women were impossibility. Pleasant's very existence offered editors a profitable contradiction. A 1891 issue of the *San Francisco Examiner* described her as "a mystery to white and colored alike, with fingers in every fortune and a devil's own luck." [18]

Such language linked racial anxiety to the era's fascination with occultism. The late nineteenth century teemed with séances and spiritualist circles; by attributing Pleasant's success to "witchcraft,"

---

[18] *San Francisco Examiner*, April 6, 1891, 3.

journalists racialized the supernatural, casting economic competence as exotic. Hudson notes that
the stereotype of the "voodoo queen" functioned
as "a secular exorcism—the city's attempt to ratio-
nalize Black female wealth through superstition."
[19]

Philanthropy and Omission

While newspapers painted her as predator, the
Black press remembered her as patron. The *Pacific Appeal* of March 1866 credited "Mrs. M.
E. Pleasant" with donations to the Colored Or-
phan Asylum and to legal defense funds. [20] Yet
even sympathetic editors avoided prolonged defense, fearing that association might taint their
own respectability politics. The result was archival
silence: the same newspapers that celebrated her
beneficence in one column ignored her defamation
in another.

The public record thus split along racial lines—white
papers inventing her, Black papers protecting her
by omission. The historian must read absence as
evidence: the quieter the coverage, the greater the
fear of contamination by proximity to power.

---

[19]Hudson, *Mammy Pleasant*, 88.
[20]*Pacific Appeal*, March 10, 1866, 2.

The Sam Davis Interview

Near the end of her life, in 1901, Pleasant granted a rare audience to journalist Sam Davis of the *San Francisco Call.* The resulting article, "The Story of Mary Ellen Pleasant," remains the closest thing to an autobiography. Davis found her living modestly in a cottage on Webster Street, surrounded by court papers and memories. His portrait vacillates between awe and condescension: "Her eyes, still keen as steel, seem to look through one's motives." [21]

She used the interview to rewrite the script. When Davis asked about her rumored sorcery, she replied, "There is no magic in business except patience." About the Bell lawsuits: "I made money for those who trusted me and trouble for those who did not." Her aphorisms were deliberate misdirection—condensed versions of decades of litigation and rumor. For the first and last time, she spoke in her own print voice, and even then she kept control of tone.

The Final Years and Obituary

When she died on January 4, 1904, at roughly ninety years of age, the same papers that had mocked her published ornate obituaries. The *San*

---

[21]Sam Davis, "The Story of Mary Ellen Pleasant," *San Francisco Call*, October 13, 1901.

Francisco Chronicle called her "a woman of mystery who moved among men of might"; the *Call* noted simply, "She was a friend of John Brown." [22] Her estate not as highly valued as the once referred to empire once measured in resentment. Friends arranged her burial at Tulocay Cemetery in Napa, marking her grave with the epitaph she had chosen years earlier.

The press, unable to resolve her contradictions, wrote them into history. In later decades, journalists and historians would resurrect her alternately as entrepreneur, spiritualist, and proto-feminist. Each retelling mirrored its moment's anxieties. What endured was not consensus but fascination, the same energy that had once turned courtroom proceedings into serialized drama.

Public Memory

Twentieth-century scholarship slowly stripped away the caricature. Works by Delilah Beasley in 1919 and by W. E. B. Du Bois in the 1920s reframed Pleasant within the lineage of Black businesswomen and abolitionists. [23] By the 1960s, her name reappeared in local commemorations as part of San

---

[22] *San Francisco Chronicle*, January 5, 1904, 7.

[23] Delilah L. Beasley, *The Negro Trail Blazers of California* (Los Angeles: Times-Mirror, 1919), 232–233; W. E. B. Du Bois, "Mary Ellen Pleasant, A Study in Contradictions," unpublished notes, Schomburg Center for Research in Black

Francisco's civil-rights heritage. Yet even celebra-
tory accounts retained the tension between myth
and evidence—an echo of the world that created
her legend to explain her success.

Pleasant's relationship with publicity thus traces
the larger history of Black women in the American
record: documented only when useful to others,
misrepresented when powerful, and rediscovered
when time made her safe. The same city that
once feared her now markets tours in her name.
Memory, too, became enterprise.

Culture.

Part III

Dangerous

Chapter 7

The Woman Who Knew Gold

Act I

By the time she stepped onto the shores of San Francisco, the verdict was she was destined to be a legend. What mattered is that she became **notorious**.

The journey west was itself a test of will. Some accounts say she sailed by way of Panama, trudging across the fever-soaked isthmus before boarding another ship bound for San Francisco. Others claim she came by Cape Horn, months of storms and starvation pressing passengers to the edge. However she traveled, she arrived not as a prospector, not as a dream-addled boy with a pan, but as a woman with sharper tools, silence, memory, and an instinct for where money pooled.

San Francisco in the early 1850s was not a city so much as a fever dream. Tents and clapboard shacks clung to hillsides like barnacles. Ships lay abandoned in the harbor, their crews vanished into the mines. The air reeked of salt, smoke, and ambition. Men boasted of nuggets the size of fists; others wept into whiskey glasses, fortunes lost before they'd even begun.

Into this chaos stepped Mary Ellen Pleasant.

She did not dig. She did not gamble on claims staked too shallow or too deep. She saw, with the clarity of a woman who had studied Nantucket's merchants, that the true gold was not in rivers but in the pockets of the men who chased them. They needed places to sleep, shirts to launder, meals to eat. They needed loans, connections, someone to steady the spinning wheel of luck.

And Pleasant knew how to provide what people needed—while keeping the ledger in her own favor.

To those who noticed her early boardinghouses and eateries, she seemed a practical entrepreneur. To those who whispered more carefully, she was something stranger: a Black woman in a city that claimed to belong to white men, moving coin with confidence, planting roots that would outlast panics and booms. She arrived without fanfare, yet her presence carried the weight of all her untraceable beginnings.

The enslaved child who learned grit in Georgia.
The apprentice who learned caution in Philadelphia.
The daughter of Haiti's mystique.
The Nantucket servant who learned the arithmetic of power.
The abolitionist who kept secrets for fugitives, who perhaps laid coins in John Brown's palm.

She carried them all ashore like invisible luggage. And San Francisco, too frantic to notice, opened its gates.

The Gold Rush was a frenzy, but for Pleasant it was opportunity: a city young enough to be shaped, raw enough to be claimed. Here, she would test whether all the rumors of her origin could be welded into a single legend. Here, she would turn silence into strategy, observation into ownership, ambiguity into empire.

She walked off the ship and into history. The cobblestones rang under her boots. The fog rolled back. Somewhere, in a parlor not yet built, someone would whisper that she was destined to be worth **thirty million dollars**.

San Francisco smelled of sweat, seawater, and dreams half-burned. The year was 1852, or thereabouts, when Mary Ellen Pleasant stepped onto its streets. She did not come clutching a miner's pan or a prospector's pick. She came with sharper instruments: memory, silence, and the instinct of a woman who had spent years studying how fortunes flowed.

The city was still raw. Hillsides teetered under shanties nailed together overnight. Gambling halls clattered with dice. Wharves groaned with ships abandoned by sailors who had bolted for the mines. Everywhere men rushed, digging, buying, selling, losing. Few paused long enough to wonder who was profiting most.

Pleasant paused. She watched. She saw that the real gold was not in the rivers but in the spaces where men collapsed at day's end: boardinghouses, kitchens, laundries. They would trade their dust for bread, their wages for beds, their dignity for a shirt clean enough to pass as new. She understood what Nantucket had already taught her: the surest profit is not in striking veins but in selling what the diggers cannot live without.

So she opened doors.

A boardinghouse first, plain wood walls but steady rent. Then another, and another. Kitchens where miners filled bowls with stew, laundries where their clothes were scrubbed raw, rooms where they laid down their heads while she tallied accounts. It was not glamourous, but it was relentless. Each coin they dropped into her palm carried a fragment of the gold they had torn from the earth.

Soon whispers followed her just as they had back east.   She was no longer the conductor of hidden routes but the keeper of visible ones -routes of commerce, of necessity.   The laundress with ledgers. The boardinghouse mistress whose profits multiplied while miners gambled theirs away.

And then there was her manner: not brash like the prospectors, not loud like the gamblers. She moved with quiet certainty, eyes sharp, voice precise. Men who laughed at first found themselves paying her rent, eating her food, wearing clothes her laundries had pressed. They realized too late that while they dug for fortune, she was already standing on it.

What made her different was not just enterprise. It was the way she blended invisibility and presence. To some she was a service worker: Mammy Pleasant, the one who fed them, clothed them, cleaned up after them. To others she was a shadowy financier, her coin sliding into investments, her hand quietly in partnerships. She let the mask shift as needed. To underestimate her was to enrich her.

By the mid-1850s, Pleasant's position was undeniable. She had not struck gold in a riverbed, but she had found the deeper seam: the city itself. San Francisco was her mine, and she extracted wealth from it with relentless precision.

And as always, rumor swelled ahead of fact. *She*

owns half the city, they whispered. *She is worth millions.* The number was not yet thirty million, but it was already myth-sized.

Act II

Success, for Mary Ellen Pleasant, was not a single stream but a braided river. The boardinghouses gave her steady profit, but she was too shrewd to stop there. San Francisco was swelling like a balloon—each new ship at the wharf meant more mouths to feed, more backs needing rest, more men dreaming of riches they would never keep. She moved quickly to claim the spaces others overlooked.

She acquired land, piece by piece, often through intermediaries who kept her name out of the records until the ink was dry. Parcels along growing streets, lots that looked worthless until the city's expansion turned them into gold. Where others saw swamps or sand, she saw inevitability. Later, when the lawsuits came, rivals sneered that she had tricked or bewitched men into selling. The truth was plainer and sharper: she simply saw further down the road than they did.

Restaurants came next: modest at first, then more ambitious. In a city of chaos, a reliable meal was treasure, and Pleasant's establishments became known for both their fare and their discretion. Hungry miners rubbed elbows with merchants, sailors, even the occasional politician. She learned who was drinking too much, who was gambling too recklessly, who was suddenly flush with dust or suddenly desperate for coin. Her kitchens fed the city, but her ears harvested it.

Streetcars were the boldest step. Public transport was the pride of San Francisco's growth, a symbol of modernity rattling along iron tracks. Pleasant saw not only a service but a stake in the city's veins. She invested quietly, threading her money into companies that thought themselves untouchable. Later, when she challenged their segregation in court, it shocked many to learn she was not merely a rider demanding justice but also a shareholder defending her own interest. That was her genius: she blurred the line between business and battle, so that each lawsuit became both civil rights case and financial maneuver.

Whispers grew louder. She was no longer just a woman with boardinghouses and laundries - she was an empire in skirts. Some claimed she owned half the restaurants along certain streets, that she held deeds in neighborhoods stretching from Nob Hill to the waterfront. The exact sums mattered less than the aura. Numbers ballooned in the telling. Five thousand became fifty. Fifty thousand became half a million. By the late 1850s, tongues were already shaping the syllables of "millions," though the exact count was lost in fog.

And Pleasant did little to correct them. She understood that wealth is not only counted but performed. A fortune is worth more if the world believes it larger than the ledger says. If rivals thought she was worth millions, they hesitated. If allies believed she was worth millions, they courted her. Either way, rumor became shield and sword.

It was here, in these years, that the outline of the thirty-million-dollar legend first appeared, faint as a watermark but growing darker with every retelling. By the time her name became synonymous with impossible wealth, the groundwork had been laid: boardinghouses, restaurants, real estate, streetcars—all of it layered atop the habits of silence and observation she had carried from Nantucket.

Mary Ellen Pleasant did not strike gold. She mined the miners. She mined the merchants. She mined the city itself.

Act III

For a time, she moved like a rumor with legs— seen everywhere, fixed nowhere. At the docks, in kitchens, in court corridors, in front parlors where men of means pretended she wasn't listening. San Francisco was not yet a city that had decided what to do with women like her. To some she was indispensable; to others, intolerable.

The newspapers tried to solve the problem of her presence by naming her. **"Mammy Pleasant,"** they called her, sketching cartoons that exaggerated her features, wrapping her ambition in the trappings of servitude. It was meant to reduce her: a caricature of the "house mammy," a relic of the Old South, stripped of menace. The editors believed that by shrinking her in ink, they could shrink her in life.

But Pleasant understood masks. She wore the name when it suited her, let it hang around her like an apron that disguised the ledger she kept beneath. If they needed to imagine her as their "Mammy," fine—she would feed them, clothe them, launder for them, all the while tallying her profits. And when the mask slipped, when her silks rustled on Nob Hill or her testimony cut through a courtroom, they discovered their mistake too late.

Her empire expanded in the shadows of these contradictions. She loaned money to men who would never publicly admit their dependence. She signed deeds that surfaced in court only years later, to the shock of rivals who had assumed she was penniless. Her reputation grew in equal parts from the wealth she accumulated and the wealth others imagined she possessed.

And then came the lawsuits.

San Francisco was a city that thrived on litigation—every claim, every contract, every promise made in whiskey had its day before a judge. Pleasant was no exception. Partners betrayed her; rivals challenged her ownership; heirs of men long dead tried to claw back fortunes they insisted she had stolen. The court dockets filled with her name.

Each case was a theater of race and gender as much as money. White men who owed her debts suddenly recalled her "dark influence." Former partners whispered of witchcraft when they could not explain their own ruin. Judges, uneasy at the sight of a Black woman wielding contracts better than barristers, dressed their prejudice in the language of skepticism.

But she did not flinch. She sat in those rooms with composure carved from Nantucket silence, letting others talk themselves into knots. Her lawyers spoke, her papers spoke louder, and though she lost as often as she won, each trial added another layer to her legend. People began to believe she could not be erased, only fought and feared.

It was during these years that the city's gossip fastened itself to a single number: **thirty million dollars.** It was repeated often enough to become fact in the minds of San Franciscans. The caricature of "Mammy Pleasant" paled beside a reported thirty-million-dollar fortune.

And Pleasant, ever the strategist, did not care what they called her.

Chapter 8

Voodoo Queen and Visionary

Act I

The fog carried her name differently now. No longer only as a landlord, a businesswoman, or a boardinghouse mistress—it carried her as something darker, something uncanny. *The Voodoo Queen of San Francisco.*

The phrase did not come from her mouth. It was a crown placed on her by enemies, a charm whispered by rivals who found no other language to explain their failure against her. When contracts favored her, they said it was not cleverness but a curse. When her fortunes multiplied, they swore she had bent unseen forces to her will. When she

appeared unshaken in court, they claimed spirits
stood beside her bench.

San Francisco was a city eager for legend. It had
sprung up almost overnight from sand dunes and
shipwrecks, a place where men swore gold nuggets
the size of fists lay just beneath the soil. A city
built on exaggeration was always ready to believe
in sorcery. Pleasant, with her quiet confidence and
her refusal to shrink, became the perfect vessel for
superstition.

They painted her as a priestess from Haiti, daughter of a conjure woman who whispered to the dead.
They said she lit candles in darkened rooms, drew
chalk symbols on the floor, tied red strings around
contracts before signing them. They imagined jars
of herbs lined like soldiers on her shelves; each one
holding a spell to ruin a rival or bless an ally.

The truth was less romantic. She kept ledgers.
She worked with clocks. Her rituals were business
habits: filing deeds before rivals thought to, paying
debts before creditors came knocking, cultivating
information in kitchens and parlors until she knew
the city better than any baron. But myth has a
way of outshouting truth.

And Pleasant understood the utility of becom-
ing the bogeywoman. She did not waste breath
denying the stories. If they wished to believe she
commanded shadows, she let them. If they trem-
bled when her name was spoken, that fear was

worth more than a lawyer's fee. Witchcraft became another mask—like "Mammy," like "Mother." A mask she allowed to remain upon her as they revealed more about their own fears than about her life.

So she walked Nob Hill streets with the composure of a Queen, while behind her shutters slammed and whispers hissed: *she is not like us; she commands something deeper.* And in that tension—between superstition and strategy—her legend swelled into something greater than either alone.

Act II

The first stories were small, almost playful. A candle glimpsed burning late in one of her boardinghouses became proof of ritual. A servant swore she heard Pleasant murmuring in a tongue not her own—never mind that it was only an account balanced under her breath. A scrap of red ribbon tied around a stack of papers was suddenly a charm to bind rivals.

The city embroidered these fragments into tapestries of fear. Soon they claimed she held séances in back rooms, that men of means came trembling to her table not for food but for prophecy. They whispered of herbs ground into powders, of dolls with pins stuck through them, of contracts sealed with curses instead of signatures. In truth, Pleasant preferred ink to incense, but San Francisco liked its stories with smoke.

Courtrooms, too, became theaters of superstition. When she appeared as plaintiff or defendant, rivals rarely confined themselves to ledgers and deeds. They spoke of her "influence," her "dark power," her "hold" over men. Some went so far as to suggest she had bewitched entire juries. Judges frowned, not because they rejected the claims, but because the suggestion that law itself might bend to sorcery unsettled even the most arrogant bench.

Yet women told different tales. Laundresses and seamstresses swore Pleasant had cured illnesses with vials of herbs, had pressed coins into widows' hands when rent was due, had whispered advice that sent a cruel landlord stumbling. To them, her power was not menace but mercy—a kind of magic that softened the sharp edges of survival. If men imagined her hexing their fortunes, women remembered her blessing theirs.

The contradiction only made her legend grow. A figure who could ruin or rescue, curse or comfort, command darkness or light. In a city obsessed with binaries—fortune and ruin, saint and sinner, gold and dirt—Pleasant became both at once.

She never confirmed these tales. She never denied them either. Instead she let them hover, knowing that myth did its own work. Fear could be as useful as respect, sometimes more. A woman accused of witchcraft is a woman others hesitate to cross. And hesitation, in business and in law, is priceless.

Thus, Pleasant allowed herself to be haunted, and to haunt in return. She let the fog cloak her as if it were incense, let the whispers paint her as conjure queen, let the contradictions coil around her until no one could separate fact from legend.

By then, the number was already spreading: **thirty million dollars.** To say she was worth such a sum was to say she must have had help from the otherworldly. To imagine her richer than the robber barons was to imagine her throne built not just on coin but on sorcery. And so the myth welded itself to the fortune, the two inseparable.

Act III

The courtroom was thick with tobacco smoke and expectation. Lawyers shuffled their papers with a flourish meant for the gallery as much as for the bench. Everyone knew this trial wasn't only about money—it was about Mary Ellen Pleasant herself.

The plaintiff's attorney rose, his voice high and theatrical, addressing not the judge but the crowd beyond the rail.
"Your Honor, we are dealing with a woman," he began, "who exerts an *unnatural* influence over men of standing. My client swears—under oath—that he was persuaded to sign away valuable property under circumstances no ordinary businesswoman could arrange."

The implication hung in the air like incense. The

word he had not said yet pressed against the walls.
Witch.

Whispers rippled through the benches. A witness
was called: a former associate, bitter, eager for the
stage. He swore that Pleasant had held him in her
drawing room past midnight, candles burning in
every corner. He insisted she whispered words he
did not understand, that the air grew heavy, that
he felt compelled to scrawl his name across the
deed as if under a spell.

The courtroom gasped. Some laughed. Others
crossed themselves.

Pleasant sat silent, her face unreadable. She did
not rise in protest, did not feed the performance
with indignation. She merely adjusted the fold of
her shawl and waited.

Her lawyer rose calmly when the witness was done.
"Compelled, you say?" he asked. "And yet the ink
on your signature dried the same as any man's.
And you cashed the payment, did you not? More
than once, you called on Mrs. Pleasant for loans.
Were those loans also the work of sorcery—or of
arithmetic?"

The gallery chuckled. The witness flushed, stam-
mered.

Pleasant's eyes never moved from him, steady as
a ledger line. The silence she cultivated did more
than her lawyer's words. It pressed the witness,

made him squirm, made the judge clear his throat impatiently.

The ruling, when it came, was prosaic: the contract stood. No magic, no hexes, only signatures and sums. But the testimony itself lingered, carried into the streets by those who preferred drama to dry legal fact. "She bewitched him," they said. "He said it under oath." The verdict mattered less than the rumor.

And so the court, meant to strip away illusions, became another stage for them.

Pleasant walked out that day as she always did: head high, steps measured, silence intact. Behind her, the whispers curled like smoke. To the city, the record now confirmed what it had always suspected: she was a woman who could bend men with unseen power.

Act IV

They told a story about a railroad magnate who mocked her at a dinner party. He was a man swollen with his own fortune, half-drunk on French wine, who laughed too loudly when her name was mentioned. "Mammy Pleasant," he jeered, raising his glass, "is no businesswoman—she is a witch. And witches burn out in the end."

The guests tittered nervously. Some eyes flicked to the doorway, half expecting her to stride in, though she was nowhere near Nob Hill that night.

Days later, the story said, the magnate's prized racehorse refused to move. It stood in its stall like a statue, eyes rolling white, muscles trembling. No whip, no spur, no coaxing could budge it. Stable-hands swore they heard a low humming sound in the air, as though the animal listened to a voice no one else could hear. The magnate cursed, pulled the reins himself, and was thrown into the dirt, his shoulder breaking in the fall.

Word spread faster than the injury healed. "She cursed him," the city whispered. "She heard his insult carried on the fog, and she answered." The horse was never the same; the magnate walked with a stoop from that day forward. Proof, people said, that Mary Ellen Pleasant's reach was longer than any lash.

Of course, no ledger records such a spell. Perhaps the horse was simply lame. Perhaps the man was too drunk to ride. But San Francisco preferred the darker tale, the one where Pleasant's silence was stronger than shouts, where insult carried a price exacted by unseen hands.

And Pleasant herself? She neither confirmed nor denied. She went about her business, her steps measured, her eyes sharp, her lips closed. By saying nothing, she let the story grow roots. She knew that fear, once planted, did not need tending—it fed itself.

And so the city spoke of her not only as landlord,

entrepreneur, or activist, but as conjurer, queen, shadow-ruler. To cross her was to risk calamity; to honor her was to hope for favor. Her fortune swelled with coin, but her legend swelled with whispers.

The two were inseparable.

Chapter 9

Dangerous

Act I

By the 1860s, Mary Ellen Pleasant was no longer merely a woman who ran boardinghouses and eateries. She was a presence threaded through San Francisco's financial veins. Her name appeared in lawsuits, on deeds, in whispers passed over brandy. Yet the city always wanted more than facts—it wanted a number.

That number became **thirty million dollars**.

No one could agree where it came from. A newspaper article hinted at it, then rivals repeated it in court, and soon it was shouted in saloons as though written in ledgers. Thirty million—more than enough to put her beside the Vanderbilts and Astors, more than enough to make her the wealthiest woman on the Pacific coast, perhaps in the nation.

The figure was impossible to prove, but that was its genius. It was too large to confirm, too intoxicating to dismiss. The rumor had the texture of truth because people wanted it to be true—or needed it to be. How else could they explain a Black woman whose power rivaled theirs?

Pleasant did not correct them. She never stood up in court or parlor to deny it. Why should she? The number served her like armor. If people believed she held thirty million, then they hesitated before crossing her. If allies thought she held thirty million, they courted her as a queen. The number itself became currency.

She invested in real estate, quietly buying properties through proxies. She slipped money into restaurants that prospered, into laundries that never lacked customers, into streetcar companies whose profits rattled along iron rails. Each coin multiplied into stories. Did she own half of Nob Hill? Was she the silent backer of a shipping firm? Did her money reach even into the mines themselves?

San Francisco's imagination did the arithmetic for her. A few thousand here became a few million there, until the sum eclipsed reality. By the time whispers reached "thirty million," the number was no longer an account—it was an incantation.

And as with all incantations, it summoned ghosts.

Some swore she kept vaults of coin beneath her houses, guarded by charms. Others insisted she stored gold bars in crates that had once carried cotton. Still others claimed she had money in New York, Boston, even London banks, her influence stretching across oceans.

The truth was likely messier, smaller, but no less remarkable. She was wealthy—wealthy enough to fight in court for years, wealthy enough to back lawsuits for civil rights, wealthy enough to haunt the imagination of a city built on speculation. But the rumor gave her something more potent than cash: the aura of untouchability.

San Francisco came to know her in two faces— *Mammy Pleasant*, the caricature meant to reduce her, and *the Woman with Thirty Million Dollars*, the legend too large to erase. Between those extremes, she carved her space.

Act II

Beneath the headlines and caricatures, another current moved—quieter, steadier, harder to trace in ink. Mary Ellen Pleasant was not only feared as a sorceress or envied as a mogul; she was remembered as a benefactor.

Among San Francisco's Black community, her name was spoken differently. She was the woman who slipped coins to keep families housed when landlords threatened eviction. The one who pressed envelopes into hands with instructions to pay lawyers' fees. The one who made sure no Black child went without schooling if she could help it.

She financed lawsuits against segregation in the city's streetcars, not just for herself but for everyone forced to stand on platforms while white passengers sat in comfort. Her persistence wore companies down until the courts finally ruled in her favor. Every clang of a streetcar bell carried the echo of her defiance.

She employed servants, cooks, and laundresses—not as disposable labor but as a network. Some were paid better than elsewhere, others given loans to start their own ventures. Pleasant understood that power was not only money in the bank but loyalty in the heart. To those who worked for her, she was not "Mammy Pleasant" but *Mrs. Pleasant*, a woman who demanded excellence and returned it with protection.

Stories multiplied. A widow said she had been on the verge of losing her home until Pleasant stepped in, quiet and stern, and arranged the mortgage. A young man remembered that she bought him books for school, urging him to study law so that one day there would be more lawyers to defend their people. A woman swore her fever broke after Pleasant gave her a vial of herbs; perhaps it was medicine, perhaps it was comfort, but either way, it was remembered as mercy.

White San Franciscans sneered at these tales or twisted them into evidence of "witchcraft." To them, generosity from Pleasant looked like manipulation, as though no Black woman could act without an ulterior spell. But for those who received her help, the label didn't matter. They knew her as a guardian, a matriarch, a benefactor who used her fortune—whatever its size—to tilt the scales, however slightly, toward justice.

In this way, the thirty-million-dollar rumor became more than armor or weapon. It became a reservoir. The legend of her wealth gave her the credibility to act, to dispense aid that carried not only money but authority. When Mary Ellen Pleasant gave you a coin, it was not just a coin—it was a sign that you stood beneath the umbrella of a woman the city whispered about in awe.

The streets may have called her a witch, but kitchens and back pews of churches called her something else: *Mother.*

Act III

Sometimes, when the city gossiped too loudly about her thirty million, Pleasant's friends told older stories. Stories from before California, before Nob Hill, before the newspapers.

They spoke of nights on the Atlantic coast, when lanterns glowed dim in Quaker kitchens, and the knock on the back door came after midnight. Pleasant would rise without a word, ushering strangers in—men with shackles still marking their wrists, women clutching children too young to understand why they must never cry out.

On Nantucket and in Boston, she had already learned how to move silently, how to make herself the seam between danger and safety. She carried messages in her eyes, not on paper. She hid fugitives in cellars and attics, pressed food into their hands, and guided them to the next safe house. She became a conductor on that secret railroad of hope, a line that stretched from plantation fields to the promise of freedom.

One story said she funneled money to John Brown himself. That she believed in him so fiercely that she risked her own fortune to fund his raid at Harpers Ferry. Historians would argue for decades whether it was true, but Pleasant never seemed concerned with proof. She claimed him proudly as a friend, a martyr, a man whose fight she shared. The truth may have been tangled in rumor, but the declaration itself was an act of courage.

Her abolitionist past cast a long shadow over her California years. When she helped Black San Franciscans fight for seats on streetcars, it was not a new impulse—it was the same fire, carried west. When she lent money to struggling families, it was the same instinct that once opened safe house doors. Her benefactions in San Francisco were echoes of lantern-lit nights on the Underground Railroad, when her fortune was not in dollars but in courage and cunning.

Thus the legend deepened. She was not only the Voodoo Queen, not only the woman rumored to hold thirty million dollars—she was also the quiet conductor who had smuggled freedom beneath the nose of tyranny. In the same breath, people could call her sorceress, benefactor, and abolitionist.

And she let them.

Because the more stories attached to her name, the more untouchable she became.

Act IV

For every rival who called her a witch, a dozen neighbors remembered her as something else. She was *Mother Pleasant*, who slipped coins into palms when wages ran thin, who stood beside young women in court when no one else would, who made sure children had books in their satchels. She was the benefactor who sent lawyers to defend the poor, who fought the indignity of segregation with stubborn persistence until the streetcars rang with freedom's bell.

For those who sat in her kitchens or worked in her houses, she was no caricature in a newspaper cartoon. She was a woman of flesh and purpose— stern, yes, but fair, demanding excellence because

she offered it herself. She was the one who remembered birthdays with gifts, who visited the
sick with herbs and encouragement, who wrote letters of introduction that opened doors otherwise
barred.

The city may have called her Mammy, witch, sorceress—
but in the parlors of San Francisco's Black community she was something greater: a baroness with
a big heart. Her wealth, whether thirty million
dollars or thirty thousand, was measured not only
in property deeds but in lives steadied, lawsuits
fought, dignity defended. She carried herself with
the authority of an empire, but her empire was
not built only on gold. It was built on people—on
loyalty, on protection, on the quiet gratitude of
those who had felt her shield.

Thus the contradiction sharpened: Pleasant the
queen of fortune, Pleasant the conjure woman,
Pleasant the mother of civil rights. She was all
of them at once, refusing to shrink to any single
story. The rumor of her billions gave her armor;
her generosity gave her soul.

By the close of the 1860s, she was no longer simply a businesswoman. She was an institution, a
myth with a heartbeat. To her enemies, she was
a shadow. To her friends, she was a mother. To
the city, she was San Francisco itself—untamed,
impossible, larger than life.

And the legend of thirty million dollars was only

beginning to tighten around her name.

Chapter 10

No Good Deed Goes Unpunished

Act I

The city that had once fed on her generosity soon found ways to sharpen it into a blade against her. Mary Ellen Pleasant had given freely: loans to partners, backing for ventures, a roof for friends, even legal aid for strangers. But favors are fragile currency. In San Francisco, gratitude had a short half-life, and debt often bred resentment faster than loyalty.

It began with whispers in the courtroom corridors. Former allies appeared now as plaintiffs. Men who had once sat at her tables accused her of trickery, coercion, even sorcery. They owed

her money, but in court they painted themselves
as victims. Women she had housed or employed
were pushed into testifying that her kindness had
strings attached, that her charity was a mask for
manipulation.

The lawsuits stacked like kindling. Each one threatened to set fire to the fortune she had built, or at
least the image of it. Judges, who had tolerated
her confidence in earlier years, now treated her
with suspicion. Lawyers sharpened their words
with venom, not only against her contracts but
against her race, her gender, her very presence in
a courtroom meant for white men of property.

And yet the cruelest irony was this: many of the
cases would not have existed had she not first
extended her hand. The loans she had given in
good faith became traps; the ventures she had
joined as a benefactor turned to accusations of
fraud when profits soured. No good deed went
unpunished.

The newspapers feasted. They described her not
as a patron but as a predator, printing caricatures
of the "Mammy Pleasant" mask twisted into a
sneer. They retold courtroom testimony with a
taste for scandal, never mind that the accusations
collapsed under the weight of evidence. Rumor
always traveled faster than verdicts.

Still, Pleasant walked into every courtroom with
the same unshaken stride. She carried herself like

a woman who had already survived worse storms. Her shawl wrapped tight, her gaze steady, she sat while men tried to undo her in words. Silence remained her sharpest weapon, forcing her accusers to stumble over their own performances while she waited for the law to grind its way toward truth.

But San Francisco was not only judging contracts. It was judging the audacity of a Black woman who had dared to rise so high.

Act II

The trials became theater, and San Francisco was hungry for a show. The city's courtrooms, once sleepy chambers for contract disputes and property squabbles, swelled into arenas where the spectacle of Mary Ellen Pleasant drew crowds as if it were opera. Clerks found themselves jostled aside by reporters carrying ink-stained notebooks, their ears pricked for the slightest phrase that could be bent into a headline. Housewives sat in the gallery beside bankers, dockworkers, and politicians, all curious to see whether the so-called "Voodoo Queen" would stumble. The law was the official business, but gossip was the true entertainment.

Each hearing opened like a play. The judge struck the gavel, the bailiff called for order, and then came the parade of former allies turned hostile witnesses. A man who had once shared her table testified with dramatic sighs that Pleasant had "ensnared" him with promises too generous to be

honest. A woman she had clothed and fed told
the jury that the kindness had been a leash, not
a gift, that charity had come laced with invisible
chains. Their words were rehearsed, polished by
counsel, dripping with the venom of betrayal. And
through it all Pleasant sat straight-backed, her
shawl pulled close, her face giving away nothing.

The accusations multiplied in shape if not in sub-
stance. One day she was accused of forging signatures: the next, of intimidating witnesses with
unseen powers. A lawyer, eager to outdo his rivals,
went so far as to suggest that Pleasant kept the spirits of Africa at her command, twisting them into
instruments of financial gain. The gallery gasped,
and the reporter's pen flew across the page. No
one bothered to ask whether such claims held up
under law; they were too valuable as stories.

The truth mattered less than the performance.
Documents and ledgers, witnesses for the defense,
even rulings in her favor often disappeared into
footnotes. What the city remembered were the
moments when a plaintiff raised his voice, when an
attorney thundered accusations of sorcery, when
the word "mammy" rolled from white lips in tones
meant to belittle. Those words printed well. Those
words stuck. In a place where fortunes were built
on gold dust and rumor, scandal was the richest
vein to mine.

Pleasant knew it. She could feel the audience as

keenly as the lawyers did. When she chose silence, it was not weakness but strategy, a refusal to join the farce on its own terms. She let the witnesses flail in their rehearsed outrage, their contradictions mounting until the air itself grew heavy with doubt. At times she answered with a single word, a clipped phrase that sliced through paragraphs of accusation. At others she sat unmoving, her gaze fixed on the judge as if daring him to weigh her in the scales of true justice rather than public appetite.

Outside the courthouse, the battle raged louder still. Newspapers feasted on her image, sketching cartoons that made her lips curl into a sinister grin, her shawl morph into the garb of a witch. Columns speculated on her "mystical influence" over the city's wealthy men, suggesting that contracts and loans were mere disguises for darker bargains. Even her victories were spun into suspicion: if she won a case, it was said to prove she had bewitched the jury; if she lost, it was offered as proof that her reign of terror was ending. Either way, her name sold papers.

Yet beneath the noise lay deeper currents. Her trials were never only about money. They were about whether a Black woman could wield wealth and authority without being cast as a villain. White men defaulted on loans every day without attracting caricatures in the press. White women ran boardinghouses, lent money, and sued debtors without

the city questioning whether they were witches.
But Pleasant's very presence at the table of power
upended San Francisco's fragile order. The lawsuits became a tool to push her back into place, to
remind her and anyone who watched that daring
too much would not go unpunished.

For Pleasant, the sting was not merely financial
but moral. Many of the plaintiffs had been friends
she had believed in, sheltered, given opportunity.
Their betrayals cut deeper than any lawyer's argument. And still, she did not weep before the crowd
or bend her spine in apology. She let the city turn
her into a villain if it must, but she would not give
it the satisfaction of her despair.

So the trials ground on, case after case, week after
week, each one more circus than judgment. To
the city they were entertainment; to Pleasant they
were endurance. And though the verdicts rose
and fell, though the accusations swelled and sub-
sided like the tides, she remained. Her silence, her
composure, her refusal to break became its own
kind of power. San Francisco would remember the
words flung against her, but it would remember
even more the image of Mary Ellen Pleasant seated
in court—unmoved, unshaken, a storm contained
within the calm of her shawl.

Act III
But flames leave scars, and in San Francisco the
smoke lingered long after the embers cooled. In-

vestors who had once lined up at her door began
to drift away. Credit that had flowed freely now
slowed to a trickle, bankers whispering excuses
about "uncertainty" and "instability," words that
masked their fear of scandal more than any true
risk of loss. Contracts she could once close with a
handshake suddenly required triple the assurances,
and even then, some partners slipped away before
ink touched paper.

Her enemies, emboldened by the courtroom theater, strutted about the city with newfound confidence. Men who had once borrowed her money
toasted her supposed ruin in parlors lit with gas
lamps, retelling the same story until it hardened
into myth: that they had bested the great Pleasant, that the Black woman who had dared to climb
above her station had finally been dragged back
to earth. Each man fashioned himself as her con-
queror, though all they had truly done was renege
on debts and sharpen lies into daggers. Still, the
city was eager to believe them. In a culture that
revered fortune yet feared those who seized it too
boldly, Pleasant's decline was a parable too deli-
cious to resist.

The whispers grew teeth. They said her fortune
was gone, that her houses stood on quicksand,
that her allies had deserted her. And yet, behind
closed doors, Pleasant kept working. She shifted
her investments, moved her capital where eyes
could not follow, leaned on the few who remained

steadfast. For every door that slammed, she found
a side entrance, a loophole, a forgotten ally willing
to honor an old debt of gratitude. The lawsuits
did not stop, but they slowed, bogged down in
endless procedure. It was as if the city itself tired
of trying to undo her and instead resigned itself to
watching whether she would unravel on her own.

But Pleasant refused to unravel. What she lost
in coin she reclaimed in legend. Each attack,
each slander, each courtroom ambush only made
her larger in the public imagination. Her name
was no longer merely that of a businesswoman or
landlady—it became a myth, a symbol, a warning.
Some whispered it with fear, others with admiration, but few in San Francisco could claim not
to know it. The very attempt to destroy her had
ensured her immortality.

Act IV

By the 1870s, Pleasant lived in a strange duality,
two women woven into one. On the streets she
was flesh and blood—an older woman wrapped in
her shawl, her gaze still sharp, her presence still
commanding. Yet in the papers and in the drawing-
room chatter she became something else entirely: a
creature of rumor, half-witch, half-queen, a figure
impossible to pin down. Reporters dubbed her
"Mammy Pleasant," a caricature meant to cage her
in stereotype, but even that mask slipped often into
something darker, more powerful, more unsettling.
To many, she was not a woman but a force.

And with that legend came danger and utility in
equal measure. White society mocked her, feared
her, sought to diminish her with ink and insult. Yet
Black San Franciscans saw in her a champion. Beneath the shadow of lawsuits and ridicule, Pleasant
poured her resources into battles that mattered:
funding civil rights cases, sheltering fugitives from
the South, mentoring Black entrepreneurs who
dreamed of carving out their own fortunes in a hostile city. While the papers obsessed over whether
she had bewitched wealthy men, she was quietly
underwriting lawsuits to desegregate streetcars and
pressing her allies to challenge discrimination in
hotels and public spaces.

Still, the punishments never ceased. No victory
in court, no vindication in law, seemed enough
to scrub away the stain her enemies had painted
across her name. If she won a case, it was whispered that she had tricked the jury; if she lost,
it was declared proof that justice itself had risen
against her. The city insisted on reading her life as
allegory, not reality: a woman too ambitious must
fall, a Black woman too wealthy must be humbled.

But Pleasant would not retreat into silence or
obscurity. If they insisted on casting her as villain,
she would inhabit the role with her own defiance.
She wrapped the caricature around her shoulders
as she wrapped her shawl, letting the myth of
"Mammy Pleasant" serve as both shield and sword.
To those who understood her true work, the mask

became a kind of camouflage, distracting enemies while she fought her deeper battles in courts and communities.

What San Francisco never grasped was that Pleasant had long ago made peace with scandal. She knew that the city judged not merely her contracts but her audacity to exist at all on its gilded stage. And so she walked forward, stride unbroken, daring the world to reckon with her presence. By then, the lawsuits were only part of the story. The larger truth was this: Pleasant had endured, and in her endurance she had transformed from woman to legend. In trying to destroy her, the city had made her unforgettable.

Part IV

Notorious

Chapter 11

Notorious

Act I

The Gold Rush had drawn fortune-seekers from every corner of the world, miners with calloused hands and broken dreams, merchants who sold more shovels than were ever swung, and speculators who gambled fortunes on whispers of veins of quartz. San Francisco swelled almost overnight into a city of tents and timber, smoke and opportunity. For Mary Ellen Pleasant, the lure of California gold was never in the streams or the soil. She understood that the real wealth of a boomtown lay in the daily needs of men too frenzied to supply themselves. Gold was not simply mined from the earth—it was scrubbed from shirts, pressed into collars, folded into the clean linens that reminded miners they were still human after weeks in the hills.

She began with a laundry, humble on its face, but
it was a keystone in disguise. From that laundry
flowed coin steadily as any vein of ore. And she
reinvested quickly, turning soap and starch into
deeds and contracts. Boarding houses followed,
each one a place where meals were served, reputations were shaped, and information was traded
over dining tables. Restaurants grew from her holdings, offering respectability to those who wished
to escape the crudeness of saloons. Then came
property—parcels in a city whose value rose by the
day, each one adding brick upon brick to the foundation of her fortune. She became indispensable
to certain circles, not because she clamored for
attention but because she moved with quiet effi-
ciency. A marriage broker here, a financial whisper
there—her matchmaking secured alliances, and in
listening to the talk of men who thought her invisible, she absorbed lessons in credit, speculation,
and investment. They believed she was only a
servant to their schemes, never noticing she was
building her own.

Yet her fortune never eclipsed her mission. The
wealth was not only for her—it became a shield
and a sword for others. In San Francisco, as in
Boston, she remained an agent of escape, one of
the West's most carefully hidden conductors of
freedom. Men and women who had fled bondage
found her door open, her purse discreetly unlocked,

her network already mapped. She placed fugitives in the houses of sympathetic whites—merchants, reformers, women with conscience enough to risk scandal. She found work in kitchens and parlors where labor would not betray them, offering stability in a city too often merciless to the vulnerable. Beneath the glittering chaos of California, she wove a parallel city, an invisible infrastructure of safety and survival.

Nor did she confine her efforts only to those who arrived from afar. California's own soil hid bondage under another name: "contracts" that were in truth chains, false papers that bound Black men and women into illegal servitude. Pleasant hunted these out, challenging them with the same ferocity she had shown back East. She knew the law well enough to weaponize it, using courts when she could, coin when she must, and reputation always. To the people she sheltered, she was not simply a benefactress but a lifeline, living proof that someone in San Francisco would not look away.

The city's streetcars became her next battlefield. At first glance, they were only vehicles—iron cars drawn on tracks, carrying passengers from one neighborhood to the next. But they were also symbols, rolling stages where citizenship was tested, dignity denied, and prejudice put on public display. Transit companies barred Black riders, enforcing a silent wall of segregation that carried humiliation in every ride refused. To be forced from a car was to be told, in front of strangers, that one's humanity stopped at the step.

Pleasant answered not with outrage alone but with calculation. She organized sit-ins before the term existed, placing herself in cars where she was not welcome, forcing drivers to decide whether they would uphold injustice in front of a crowd. She used her own body as argument, her presence as protest. When companies still refused, she took the fight where she was strongest: the law. In 1866, after being forcibly ejected from a North Beach and Mission Railroad car, she filed suit. The case wound its way through delays and resistance, but Pleasant was patient. She knew change did not arrive quickly, and she had built her life on endurance.

Two years later, the California Supreme Court upheld her claim. It was not total victory—segregation did not vanish overnight—but it was a crack in the wall, a precedent that could not be erased. An early tremor, small but undeniable, in a system that believed itself immovable. Her lawsuit became a marker that others could point to, a foothold for the next climb. And though it would take another quarter-century before California formally outlawed streetcar segregation in 1893, that victory bore the imprint of Mary Ellen Pleasant's hand. She had sat where she was not allowed, spoken when she was not supposed to, and forced the state itself to listen.

Act II

Pleasant's victory on the streetcars should have crowned her with honor. She had taken on a corporation, pressed her case through the courts, and altered the legal landscape of California. For any other reformer, such an achievement might have guaranteed a legacy of respect, a place in the annals of progress beside men who were lauded for far less. But Mary Ellen Pleasant was not "any other reformer." She was a Black woman who had amassed wealth, power, and influence in a city that could not stomach the sight of her at the summit. And so the laurels of victory were swiftly braided into thorns.

The newspapers that might have praised her instead sharpened their pens. They called her audacious, unnatural, dangerous, never courageous as she truly was. Her work on behalf of fugitives and illegally enslaved Californians was twisted into suspicion: if she sheltered people, surely, she must be hiding darker dealings; if she provided jobs, surely she was running brothels under the guise of boarding houses. Even the same establishments that white patrons had once praised as respectable were suddenly derided as dens of vice when linked to her name. The double standard was blatant. What was shrewd in a white man became deceit in Mary Pleasant.

Respectability, that fickle currency of the nineteenth century, was denied to her at every turn.
The city's elites, who had benefited from her matchmaking, her capital, her counsel, now whispered
that she had overstepped. To walk into court with
dignity, to ride a streetcar in defiance, to lend
money with the authority of a banker—each act
was cast not as progress but as threat. They could
not undo her victories, so they set out to tarnish
her reputation, a quieter kind of violence but no
less destructive.

And yet Pleasant persisted. She did not retreat
into silence or hide behind her wealth. She moved
through the city with her shawl drawn close, still
funding lawsuits, still opening doors for those who
needed refuge, still pressing against the boundaries
that hemmed her people in. If San Francisco insisted on turning her into a scandal, she would
outlast the scandal. If they insisted on painting
her as villain, she would not shrink from the mask.
The streetcar fight had taught her something enduring: even partial victories left cracks in the
wall, and cracks had a way of spreading.

Act III

Even as she carved victories on the streets of San
Francisco, Pleasant's name carried the shadow of
Harpers Ferry. John Brown's failed raid in 1859
had shaken the nation, a flash of gunpowder and
prophecy that convinced some slavery could never
be ended without blood. For decades afterward,

to align with Brown was to step into dangerous territory—hero to some, traitor to others, fanatic to many. Mary Ellen Pleasant did not flinch. She claimed him.

Stories spread that she had given him money, not in small sums but in a torrent—thirty thousand dollars, an amount that in today's measure swells toward a million. Whispers linked her to the anonymous note found in Brown's pocket after his hanging, a scrap of paper that read like scripture for revolution: *"The ax is laid at the foot of the tree. When the first blow is struck, there will be more money to help."* Historians have never proven the handwriting, but Pleasant herself admitted in later years that she was the wealthy Northerner who had promised such aid. In claiming the legend, she made it truth enough.

For San Franciscans already suspicious of her, the connection was dynamite. To them she was not just a businesswoman or benefactress but a conspirator in treason, a woman who had financed insurrection with coin minted in the very system she sought to destroy. The newspapers leaned hard on the rumor, sketching her not only as Mammy Pleasant but as the witch behind John Brown's gallows. To fund such a man was to confess that she believed slavery could not be debated away, could not be compromised out of existence, but must be torn up by the root.

And that was exactly what she believed. Pleasant never softened her words about Brown. She called him comrade, martyr, proof that freedom was not free. In this, she scandalized not only San Francisco but much of the nation, which preferred its reformers tame and its Black women silent. Yet Pleasant refused to trade reverence for safety. If the choice was to be remembered as radical or not at all, she would take radical every time.

In tying her name to Brown, she also tied California to the larger story of abolition. She reminded the West—so eager to present itself as detached from the nation's civil war—that slavery's shadow reached all the way to its golden hills. Her work in boarding houses, in courtrooms, on streetcars, all stood within that same current of struggle. Brown had swung an axe at the tree; she had kept swinging, if with different tools.

Act IV

Pleasant's battles did not end with streetcars or whispers of John Brown. In the 1880s she became entangled in one of the most sensational trials of the century: *Sharon v. Sharon.* Sarah Althea Hill, the mistress of Senator William Sharon, claimed she was his secret wife. Sharon called her nothing more than a companion paid by contract—five hundred dollars a month to keep her company, occasionally in his bed. Pleasant sided with Hill, paying her legal fees and lending counsel when the young woman's voice would have otherwise been drowned by the Senator's influence. To Pleasant, the contract looked like marriage in disguise, stripped of dignity and tossed aside when it no longer served Sharon's ambition.

The trial became national theater. David Terry, one of Hill's lawyers, fell into the case with the fervor of a man too entangled, eventually marrying Hill himself. Sharon's defenders accused Pleasant of sinister manipulation, suggesting she had orchestrated the case for her own dark designs. Reporters salivated over the story, weaving tales of poisoned food and whispered spells, reducing her support for Hill to superstition and malice. On the stand, however, Pleasant confounded them all. She was articulate, measured, consistent—neither the kindly "mammy" nor the conniving witch the city had painted, but a strategist speaking truth in a room hostile to her presence. The verdict fell against Hill, and when Terry erupted in rage, Justice Stephen J. Field sentenced him to six months in jail. A year later, Terry was killed by Field's own bodyguard. The press declared Pleasant's reputation ruined, but in San Francisco, where memory of her civil rights battles still lingered, respect did not vanish so easily.

Her later years centered on the Bell mansion, a 30-room house spanning two city blocks, a kingdom of sorts that she shared with the family of financier Thomas Bell. There, fifteen souls lived under one roof: the Bells, their children, Pleasant

herself, servants, and even a young Native cou-
ple. Pleasant managed not only the household but
the fortunes—Bell's wealth mingled with her own,
transactions so intertwined that it was hard to
say where one ended and the other began. Teresa
Bell, Thomas's wife, accepted the arrangement un-
easily, asking Pleasant for money and watching her
consult Thomas before any request was granted.

When Thomas Bell fell to his death in 1892, the
foundation of that kingdom cracked. Teresa, given
to instability, accused Pleasant of theft, of manipulation, of having bent her husband to her will.
Courts pored over ledgers and deeds, trying to un-
tangle years of shared investments. Pleasant could
prove she had paid for the mansion's construction,
but it was no longer enough. Teresa pressed her
claims, and by decade's end Pleasant was forced
to leave the house she had built. She moved into
a modest apartment on Webster Street, cash-poor
though not destitute, still holding scattered investments, still willing to fight.

Even then, she did not surrender. She filed suit to
recover her property, including a prized collection
of diamonds. She gave generously when she could—
donating the equivalent of ten thousand dollars to
found Saint Mary's College in the same year her
creditors declared her insolvent. She entered her
last years in battle, her name still in the courts,
her legend still alive in the streets. The cases were
not settled by the time she died, but the record

remains: she had lived boldly, fought fiercely, and
left scars on the law itself.

Chapter 12

She is Legend

Act I

By the close of the nineteenth century, Mary Ellen Pleasant had outlived many of her allies and nearly all of her enemies. Age crept upon her like a tide, yet her resolve did not recede. The woman who had once overseen a thirty-room mansion on two city blocks now lived in a modest six-room apartment on Webster Street. The newspapers made a spectacle of this downsizing, framing it as the fall of a woman who had "risen too high." They described her as a relic of another age, their words dripping with the smugness of those who mistake reduced fortune for defeat. But Pleasant had never measured herself in the shallow scales of society gossip.

Though cash-poor in her final decade, she was never truly destitute. She still held scattered investments, small streams of income from properties and ventures she had stitched together over years. She continued to pursue her legal battles, most notably for the return of her jewels—a collection of diamonds whose brilliance symbolized not just wealth but endurance. She gave when she could, donating generously to causes like the founding of Saint Mary's College, even as courts declared her insolvent. Few would have faulted her for turning inward, hoarding what little remained. Instead, she kept to the same habit that had defined her life: using whatever she had to strengthen others.

In her twilight years she was often seen walking the streets of San Francisco, wrapped in her shawl, her carriage still upright, her gaze still steady. Children whispered that she was a witch. Old acquaintances whispered that she was ruined. But those who knew her, those who had once benefited from her hand, saw something else entirely: a woman who had survived slander, betrayal, and the grinding machinery of a city determined to break her. She had stepped into San Francisco as a force of will, and even as her body grew frail, the force never left.

Act II

When Pleasant died in 1904, San Francisco was not the same city she had entered at the height of the Gold Rush. The raw mining camp of tents and saloons had become a metropolis of banks, theaters, and steel-ribbed ambition. The city had grown, but it had grown in her shadow. Few in power would admit it, but her presence had altered the moral landscape. She had forced the courts to acknowledge Black testimony, fought the transit companies into legal submission, and made it possible for fugitives from slavery to find work and shelter far from the lash. These were not small victories; they were tectonic shifts.

For African Americans in San Francisco, Pleasant was not just a benefactor but a blueprint. She had shown that it was possible to carve out a place in a city that was both dazzling and hostile. Her boarding houses, laundries, and restaurants had offered more than wages; they had offered stability, dignity, and community. They were, in essence, a prototype of what later generations would call "Black Wall Street." Tulsa would rise decades later as a beacon of Black wealth, but in San Francisco, long before, Pleasant had already demonstrated the principle: collective advancement rooted in enterprise, guarded by courage, and fueled by vision.

Her work lingered in subtle ways. The Black men and women who walked freely onto a streetcar after 1893 did so in the wake of her defiance. The laborers who earned honest pay in her establishments carried the echo of her investment. Even those who had never met her directly knew her as a story, an example passed in church pews, parlors, and kitchen tables: if Pleasant could challenge the system and force it to bend, then so could others. Her life became a kind of parallel constitution, written not in statutes but in acts of defiance and resilience.

Act III

Pleasant's impact did not end with her passing. Death closed her eyes but could not silence her imprint. Her story became the soil from which future generations rooted their own challenges to injustice. She had tilled that ground with her lawsuits, watered it with her wealth, and fortified it with her relentless will. Long after her body was laid to rest, the seeds she planted kept sprouting in unexpected places—in the speeches of young reformers, in the strategies of Black entrepreneurs, in the determination of community organizers who knew her name only as legend yet carried her methods like instinct. Every Black lawyer who entered a San Francisco courtroom to argue for civil rights stood on the ground she had cleared, whether or not they traced their footsteps back to her. Every entrepreneur who dared to open a business in a city eager to strip away their legitimacy was echoing her blueprint, even if they never saw the lines she first drew. Pleasant had shown them the tools: money as shield, reputation as sword, law as battlefield. Others learned to wield them, and the echoes of her defiance became part of the West's political grammar.

Her work in California's version of the Underground Railroad, quieter than her lawsuits, left an equally profound legacy. History tends to honor the thunderclaps—court cases, verdicts, riots—but Pleasant's genius thrived in the silences between. She demonstrated that resistance could bloom in the hidden corners of the city: in drawing rooms where fugitives passed as servants, in boarding houses where runaways were given new names, in kitchens where food was shared and trust was earned. She proved that freedom did not always arrive with banners flying; sometimes it was smuggled across thresholds in the middle of the night. This lesson endured: that liberation is sustained as much by networks of care as by public protest, that the small hands of many could weave a safety net strong enough to defy the law. Community networks, covert aid, and mutual support became the backbone of Black survival in the West, and Pleasant's fingerprints lingered on each strand of that fabric.

Perhaps her greatest gift was the permission she embodied. She lived without waiting for the gatekeepers of white society to grant her entry. She never asked for recognition before she built, defended, and expanded. In doing so she redefined the very terms of legitimacy. Her audacity became contagious. Young women, especially, looked to her example and saw that defiance could wear a shawl, that power could be cloaked in silence, that leadership was not limited to pulpits or podiums. She taught by living that one did not need to be invited to history's table—one could build a table of one's own and make others take notice.

Later activists in California and beyond drew strength from her memory. The desegregation battles of the twentieth century echoed the strategy she pioneered: lawsuits paired with community organizing. When San Francisco schools and public spaces were pressed to integrate, the legal and tactical playbook bore traces of her. Labor organizers in Oakland, Los Angeles, and San Francisco adopted her blend of economic leverage and political resistance, recognizing—as Pleasant had—that wealth, pooled and wielded collectively, could be a weapon against exclusion. The rise of the Black Panther Party in Oakland during the 1960s carried forward her philosophy in new form. Their survival programs—free breakfasts, community health clinics, mutual aid networks—were modern descendants of her boarding houses, her job placements, her insistence that freedom was not abstract but lived in the body and the home. Pleasant had proved a century earlier that Black power was not only a slogan; it was a practice, grounded in economics, law, and daily survival.

And here lies the bridge: from shawl to leather jacket, from whispered networks to shouted manifestos, from court petitions in the 1860s to chants in the streets a century later. Pleasant was California's prophetic ancestor, standing at the head of a lineage of defiance that stretched from Gold Rush laundries to Oakland rallies. When the Panthers demanded community control of schools, when Angela Davis raised her voice in San Jose and beyond, when Black entrepreneurs carved wealth from hostile markets in the Bay Area, they were standing on ground Pleasant had already claimed. Her presence became a kind of spiritual infrastructure for resistance in California.

She had already proven that one woman could wield wealth against prejudice, that one lawsuit could dismantle a system of humiliation, that one life could become a lever against the machinery of injustice. The Panthers, the NAACP lawyers, the Black business owners of the West Coast—all carried, knowingly or not, her fire.

And so she remains more than memory. She is blueprint, she is foundation, she is the quiet force behind the many battles that came after. Her life whispered to the generations that followed: *Do not wait to be accepted. Stand, build, fight, endure. Make the world answer to you.*

Act IV

Over time, the cruel caricature of "Mammy Pleasant"— that grotesque mask of derision the newspapers had once forced upon her—has slowly fallen away. For decades, that image lingered: a distorted sketch of a woman reduced to stereotype, vilified for her defiance, mocked for her independence, turned into a villain in the public imagination. The press had painted her as a manipulator, a witch, a brothel-keeper, anything but the strategist and benefactor she truly was. That caricature clung stubbornly, because it was easier for society to belittle her than to admit she had bested them in their own arenas—courtrooms, contracts, politics, and power. Yet history is relentless. What scandal once shouted has grown faint with time, while the quieter truths of her legacy have grown louder. What had once been a smear has been replaced by remembrance.

Today, San Francisco carries her name in places where people gather and breathe. A city park— Mary Ellen Pleasant Memorial Park—offers shade under trees where children play and elders rest. For many who pass through it, the name is a curiosity, a marker on a signpost. For others, especially those who know her story, it is a reclaimed altar. It reminds the city that beneath its gilded past of gold and commerce, there lived a woman who bent the law and wealth toward justice. To sit in that park is, in some small way, to sit in the presence of her persistence.

At the corner of Octavia and Bush streets, a plaque rests where her thirty-room mansion once commanded attention. The house itself—an empire of stone, timber, and ambition—was lost to time, but the ground still remembers. The plaque does more than mark geography; it testifies. It says that here, in this place, lived a woman who re-shaped the destiny of others. Passersby who pause to read encounter not the lurid tales of her critics but the recognition of her achievements. The city that once smeared her has, in fragments, admitted its debt.

Her story also circulates in classrooms, where history teachers lift her name beside those of Frederick Douglass and Harriet Tubman. She is studied in historical societies, where archives reveal not the sensational rumors but the contracts, letters, and lawsuits that prove her strategy. More importantly, her story lives in the oral traditions of Black San Franciscans. In church basements, community meetings, and family kitchens, her name is spoken not as gossip but as inheritance. She is called the Mother of Civil Rights in California, not out of courtesy, but because she earned the title in courts, in homes, and in the streets of a hostile city.

The shift from scandal to testament is not accidental— it is the work of memory reclaimed. For much of the twentieth century, history books ignored her or repeated the slanders of her enemies. But communities refused to forget. They told her story in whispers at first, then in louder voices, until scholars began to take notice, until markers were erected, until her place in history could no longer be denied. In this way, Pleasant's legacy mirrors her life: she forced her way into spaces that tried to exclude her. Even in memory, she had to fight for her rightful seat.

Now, what had once been whispered as scandal is spoken as testament. Each retelling adds weight to her true identity. Each monument pushes the caricature farther into irrelevance. Where the newspapers of her day tried to cage her in ridicule, the city now honors her with stone, metal, and living memory. She has become more than the controversies that dogged her. She is remembered as strategist, entrepreneur, abolitionist, civil rights pioneer.

And yet, there is something fitting in this evolution. Pleasant knew better than most that reputation is a battlefield. She watched her name weaponized against her, turned into caricature, wielded as scandal. But just as she endured the courtrooms and betrayals of her time, her legacy has endured the distortions of history. She outlived her enemies in life, and she has outlasted them in memory.

Her park, her plaque, her presence in the city's stories—these are not just memorials. They are reclamations. They are San Francisco's belated admission that Mary Ellen Pleasant cannot be confined to insult, cannot be erased by scandal, cannot be reduced to a mask. She remains, and she remains larger than her detractors ever imagined.

What had once been whispered in shame is now

spoken with reverence. What had once been caricature is now canon. What had once been scandal
is now scripture in the book of California's long
struggle for justice.

Mary Ellen Pleasant has become what she always
was ... **a legend.**

Act V

Over the years, Pleasant's life has been retold
and reimagined through film, television, books,
performance, poetry, and art. The caricature of
"Mammy Pleasant" has been steadily replaced with
a fuller portrait, one that emphasizes her abolitionist courage, her business genius, and her role
as the Mother of Civil Rights in California.

She has been the subject of documentaries, including *Meet Mary Pleasant*, a PBS "ViewFinder"
episode profiling her abolitionist work and legacy
(2023), and *Meet Mary Pleasant* (2008), a TV
film narrated by Ruby Dee.[1] Local institutions
such as the San Francisco Public Library have
also screened films like *The Legacy of Mary Ellen
Pleasant*, reinforcing her role as a civic icon.[2] More
recently, her entrepreneurial side was examined in
the 2023 podcast *Drapetomaniax: Unshackled History*, in an episode entitled *Mary Ellen Pleasant:
Black Capitalist*.[3]

Scholars and authors have explored her life in
depth. Sue Bailey Thurman's *Pioneers of Ne-*

gro Origin in California (1952) was among the earliest works to preserve her legacy in print.[4] Lynn Hudson's *The Making of "Mammy Pleasant"* (2003) investigates how myth and prejudice obscured her contributions.[5] Susheel Bibbs' *Heritage of Power* (2012) combines scholarship with performance to reclaim her voice.[6] Shomari Wills includes her in *Black Fortunes* (2018), situating her among the first African American millionaires.[7] Literary imagination has also embraced her: Angela Davis praised *Free Enterprise: A Novel of Mary Ellen Pleasant* for blending fact with creative reconstruction, giving Pleasant a space in historical fiction.[8]

Her image has inspired poetry, visual art, and community exhibits. Cheryl Derricotte has created book-arts projects such as *The Autobiography of the Late Mary Ellen Pleasant* and *21 Lessons on Freedom, Love, and Money*, which fold her story into tactile, visual form.[9] Bay Area exhibitions like *Collecting Arising: The Insistence of Black Bay Area Artists* have placed Pleasant's legacy within a continuum of Black creativity and resistance.[10] Oral traditions and poetry within San Francisco's Black community also keep her alive, affirming her as both ancestor and symbol.

The lasting impact of these representations is twofold. First, they reclaim her reputation from the racist distortions of her lifetime, recasting her not as caricature but as pioneer. Second, they embed her story into the larger American cultural imagination. She expands the timeline of civil rights beyond the mid-twentieth century, reminding audiences that legal resistance, economic empowerment, and social defiance were being practiced by Black women generations earlier. By inspiring writers, artists, filmmakers, and historians, Pleasant has secured a place not only in the annals of law and abolition but in the living archive of American media itself.

Part V

Appendix

Chronological Timeline of Mary Ellen Pleasant

c. 1814   **Birth and early years.** Likely
August 19, 1814; later self-report
names Philadelphia, while other accounts suggest Georgia/Louisiana.
Raised for a time on Nantucket in
the Quaker Hussey household; learned
literacy, bookkeeping, and disciplined
discretion.[1]

1830s–1840s **Abolitionist networks.** Works
in New England reform circles; mar-
ries James Smith, a prosperous free
Black contractor in Boston. Their
home functions as an Underground

---

[1] Lynn M. Hudson, *The Making of "Mammy Pleasant"*
(Urbana: University of Illinois Press, 2003), 3–8.

Railroad station.[2]

1850   **Fugitive Slave Act.** Federal law criminalizes assistance to fugitives; Pleasant continues clandestine financing of escapes and aligns herself with militant abolitionists in principle and, by later claim, in fact.[3]

1852   **Migration West.** After Smith's death, sails to California (via Panama or Cape Horn, sources vary). Arrives in San Francisco during peak Gold Rush commerce; invests in boardinghouses, kitchens, and laundries.[4]

1850s   **Enterprise and capital.** Expands establishments; begins quiet partnerships (notably with banker Thomas Bell) to hold real estate and other investments by proxy.[5]

1858–1859   **John Brown connection.** Later recounts aiding Brown "with my last dollar and my last prayer," link-

[2]John William Templeton, *Our Roots Run Deep: The Black Experience in California, 1500–1900* (San Francisco: ReUNION, 1991), 87–89.

[3]Hudson, *The Making of "Mammy Pleasant"*, 27–29.

[4]Delilah L. Beasley, *The Negro Trail Blazers of California* (Los Angeles: Times-Mirror, 1919), 56–57.

[5]Hudson, *The Making of "Mammy Pleasant"*, 53–59.

ing her legacy to the Harpers Ferry martyrdom and militant abolitionism.[6]

1860s **War years, west coast.** Accumulates wealth through property, transport, and food service; supports Unionist and Black communal efforts. Public rumor inflates her fortune into the multi-million range.[7]

1866–1868 **Streetcar civil-rights suits.** Helps file/finance cases against segregation: *Pleasant v. North Beach & Mission Railroad Co.* (1866) and *Pleasant v. Omnibus Co.* (1868), contributing to desegregation precedents in California transit.[8]

1870s **Notoriety and masks.** Newspapers push the racist sobriquet "Mammy Pleasant"; rivals allege "witchcraft." She continues business and targeted philanthropy despite smear campaigns.

---

[6]Hudson, 47–48.

[7]Kevin Starr, *Americans and the California Dream, 1850–1915* (New York: Oxford University Press, 1973), 52–54.

[8]William C. Beecher, "Mary Ellen Pleasant and the California Streetcar Cases," *California Legal History* 7 (2012): 121–133.

1875–1880   **Estate entanglements.** After Thomas Bell's accidental death (1876), prolonged litigation over assets and influence; significant legal costs and adverse rulings erode net worth.[9]

1880s   **Decline and endurance.** Ongoing suits and expenses diminish holdings; remains a force in San Francisco's Black community via employment support and legal aid funds.

1904   **Death.** January 4, San Francisco (about age 90). Buried at Tulocay Cemetery, Napa. Epitaph chosen by friends: *"She was a friend of John Brown."*[10]

Legacy   **Afterlife of a legend.** Reassessed as an early self-made Black millionaire and western civil-rights pioneer; scholarship continues to parse myth versus documentation.[11]

---

[9]Hudson, *The Making of "Mammy Pleasant"*, 95–102.

[10]Beasley, *Negro Trail Blazers*, 233.

[11]Hudson, *The Making of "Mammy Pleasant"*, ix–xiii; Stacey L. Smith, *Freedom's Frontier* (Chapel Hill: University of North Carolina Press, 2013), 272–275.

Endnotes

1. *Meet Mary Pleasant*, PBS ViewFinder, Season 5, Episode 6 (2023); *Meet Mary Pleasant*, TV Movie, narrated by Ruby Dee (2008), IMDb

2. San Francisco Public Library, "The Legacy of Mary Ellen Pleasant" (Film Screening, 2024).

3. *Drapetomaniax: Unshackled History*, Episode: "Mary Ellen Pleasant: Black Capitalist" (2023).

4. Sue Bailey Thurman, *Pioneers of Negro Origin in California* (Boston: Chapman & Grimes, 1952).

5. Lynn Hudson, *The Making of "Mammy Pleasant": A Black Entrepreneur in Nineteenth-Century San Francisco* (Urbana: University of Illinois Press, 2003).

6. Susheel Bibbs, *Heritage of Power: Mary

Ellen Pleasant (Oakland: MEP Publications, 2012).

7. Shomari Wills, *Black Fortunes: The Story of the First Six African Americans Who Escaped Slavery and Became Millionaires* (New York: Amistad, 2018).

8. Jewelle Gomez, *Free Enterprise: A Novel of Mary Ellen Pleasant* (San Francisco: City Lights, 2004).

9. Cheryl Derricotte, *The Autobiography of the Late Mary Ellen Pleasant* and *21 Lessons on Freedom, Love, and Money,* artist book projects (2018–2019).

10. "Collecting Arising: The Insistence of Black Bay Area Artists," exhibit featuring works tied to Pleasant's legacy, Napa, CA (2023).